Dating, Intimacy

& the

Teenage Years

Dating, Intimacy

& the

Teenage Years

Karl Duff

Treasure House

An Imprint of

Destiny Image® Publishers, Inc.
P.O. Box 310
Shippensburg, PA 17257

"For where your treasure is,
there will your heart be also." Matthew 6:21

ISBN 1-56043-131-8
(Previously published as *Teens, Sex & Happiness*)

For Worldwide Distribution
Printed in the U.S.A.

Revised Edition: 2001

This book and all other Destiny Image, Revival Press,
MercyPlace, Fresh Bread, Destiny Image Fiction,
and Treasure House books are available
at Christian bookstores and distributors worldwide.

For a U.S. bookstore nearest you, call **1-800-722-6774**.
For more information on foreign distributors, call **717-532-3040**.
Or reach us on the Internet: **www.reapernet.com**.

Contents

Introduction

A re you a teen? Perhaps; but you may also be a parent or a teacher. Either way, what are the purpose and ideas of this book on sex? How are they taught? How can they best be reinforced by teens or those who love teens?

Pre-marital sex is rapidly destroying an entire society. No! It is destroying an entire civilization and drawing millions back to a pagan and satanic world view. The convenience of sex in every form on TV and among friends and the acceptance of it by the world as "okay as long as nobody gets hurt" is causing a vast world of extreme hurt. Too late do those deceived realize it. In addition to the death *of a majority of marriages,* sometimes 15-25 years later, ruination by sexual immorality passes iniquity onto the children of such marriages. Also, pre-marital sex has now led to a whole "death" mentality regarding the value of life, destroying millions of pre-born babies.

So far, there has been a notable lack of power to protect young people from "blowing" their lives for the momentary pleasure of pre-marital sex.

Let there be no misunderstanding about who is responsible for failure of morality before marriage. It is basically the fault of men: fathers and boys who never became men because they were led to live part of their lives in secret (like masturbation) and thought that sex with anyone is "okay." Did I say "anyone"? Well, maybe some have believed instead that sex before marriage with someone you "love" is "okay."

But it isn't. Pre-marital sex has devastating consequences for both girls and boys. This book shows why by explaining the different destructions that result in each. It also singles out the *lie* that sucks both into destruction, and it uses the vision God has given to youth to help them understand the *truth* and the *lie* about love and sex.

One thing youth has in abundance is a capacity for *vision*. God has built into both boys and girls a vision of what is required to find happiness in marriage. This book takes as its basis the natural vision of each by gender and relates it motivationally to (a) the plan of God leading to marriage and (b) the gospel of Jesus Christ—the same vision according to the Word of God.

Do young people really have vision? Ask any boy who has been to summer camp and who aspires to the adventure, quest, and recognition of becoming an Eagle Scout. (There may be little to draw boys into a renewed vision after 17 or 18 years of age, but it is not a problem at age 12!) Ask any girl who dreams of being a wife and a mother.

Girls have a more detailed vision than boys and they receive it earlier in life. This vision is a powerful motivation for finding the man whom God has sent, and it remains vivid unless a girl is ruined by a man or boy. A girl's vision is a key to her happiness. Boys also have a vision. They know in their hearts that they were destined for something great, which then eludes many of them their whole life. What is it?

These visions are all from God, and this book is a reinforcement of these visions.

Vision and *truth* are powerful vaccinations against darkness and lies. When they are brought into the light, satan has little room to hide. If parents have the option, they can enhance this vaccinating power by staying close beside their children while this information is digested.

My wife and I used to read to our children at the dinner table after dessert. When the kids got old enough to read, we let them take a turn. One chapter per evening was about the norm.

This book is designed to be read one chapter per day and then discussed, individually or with others. Discussion and re-reading will more than double the amount of truth that "sticks" with each person. Two months would be a good leisurely rate to digest the thirty-six chapters.

Older teens and youth groups may not want to read with another person, but I hope you, too, will work at the discussion questions. *Test what your spirit is saying before you read ahead.* I think you'll be amazed by the power of your discernment.

Those portions that are truly from God will be established anyway, whether or not you follow these suggestions. They carry God's anointing and power. Yet I hope you'll discuss the questions to receive maximum benefit.

It is God's desire that all the young may be secure in their hopes for the future, to know that God is on their side with a plan. He wants to demonstrate power on their behalf and assure them that there is an unseen world in which their *bridegroom* has battled for them and won. His purposes of happiness will be accomplished in all our young people who pursue Him and His vision.

**The Knight in Shining
Armor**

A Daughter's Vision

Every young girl has a great vision for her future. This vision usually includes marriage to a man who will be everything she desires and a happy home that is blessed with children. Unfortunately, some girls never obtain this goal because things mess up their hopes.

This book is for every girl who dreams of a happy future. I hope all who read it will learn how to safeguard their fondest hopes and dreams from getting messed up. Nearly always, it is a boy who destroys a girl's hopes. This boy may be a boyfriend, a brother, or even a father who never grew up. Usually a girl's hopes are shattered by a boyfriend when she gets involved with him in the wrong way as she tries to help her dreams come true.

Although some girls may never discuss their dreams with their fathers, mothers, or girlfriends, most girls dream of the same thing. Each longs for a boy who will love her so much that he is willing to do anything to win her love and protect her. She thinks in terms of a knight in shining armor who will rescue her from a castle or slay the dragon that imprisons her. Even though this dream may sound like a fairy tale, much like "Snow White" or "Beauty and the Beast," it is not foolish because it comes straight from the heart of *God*. This picture is His vision for all girls!

We all love stories of heroes who rescue their sweethearts, girls whom they will cherish for life. These are the stories that become classics. Although some of these stories have been made popular by Walt Disney, the tales they tell are not new. Instead, they reflect what is already true. *The stories did not come first. The truth given by God as a vision for each girl's heart came first!* The stories merely describe the truth and the vision God planned for men and women.

God *intends* for each girl to have a man who is willing to die to win her love and happiness. *He* is the source of the dreams that fill young girls' hearts. There are problems, though, in seeing this vision come true. What God intends is not always what happens. Foolishness is at work in the hearts of all the boys every young girl meets. Foolishness is also at work in the heart of every young girl. How can boys and girls, young men and young women, work together with *God* to avoid the pitfalls of this foolishness?

Things to Think About

1. Did you see the movie *Beauty and the Beast* (or have you read the story)?

2. What did you like about the Beast?

3. What do you think the girl liked about the Beast?

4. Do boys also have a vision?

A Boy's Desire

Boys don't really have visions in the same manner as girls. As we will see later, boys don't "see" things *inside* themselves like girls do. Instead, they tend to look at things *outside* themselves. Yet, boys still have desires, one of the greatest of which is to be heroic. They want to do something great. In fact, boys have a sort of built-in knowledge that they are destined to do something great.

What does it mean to do *something great*? Most boys don't know. So here is a big problem. Boys know that they want to achieve something great, but they don't know what to do or how to do it. Thus, they simply act instinctively. Usually this means that they try to do something that will win high approval from others.

If boys really thought about it, they would agree that they want to be recognized for having courage, for doing something well that is hard to do, or for possessing a good character trait. Too often, however, boys miss these goals because they are too shallow. Instead of doing something great that will gain them positive recognition, they end up doing practically anything that gets attention from others.

Thus, it is easy to draw boys into nearly anything that will gain attention from others. They will compete in games, they will show off, they will tease, they will compete athletically, they will pull pranks and tell jokes—all to get attention. Rarely are their exploits difficult or courageous, nor do they bring out an admirable character trait. Because they are still boys, they act like boys.

Both boys and girls recognize that a boy's doing something great may be connected with overcoming fear. (We will see why later.) Hence, boys are easily drawn into doing foolish things. Their desire to be recognized—even if this means being the best at being "bad"—overrides their common sense and compels them to do things that are downright mean, rude, or dangerous. Still, God puts into boys this desire to do great things, and He wants to use it for good.

Girls, because they are looking for boys who are willing to take risks and who have the courage to be heroes on their behalf—that is, to do what is right or to help them in a right way—are easily deceived into admiring a foolish boy who has earned a reputation. Even a bad reputation seems to make a boy important. Thus, girls sometimes go for a boy who receives much attention from others, or who other girls think is important, even though that boy may have no real courage or character. This encourages the boy's irresponsible actions because he is getting what he desires—attention.

This nature of boys to reach for something great reflects God's design for male human beings. He created boys to grow into men who can face danger and do great things for Him. He gave them competitive traits that will enable them to be successful men and successful husbands. It also goes with the visions of girls that we talked about in the last chapter. God intends that the dreams of girls and the desires of boys will work together. But this happens in a totally different way than you might expect.

Things to Think About

1. In the story or movie *Beauty and the Beast*, what was the difference between the Beast and the evil Gaston, who also wanted the girl?

2. Do you see people around you who are like Gaston or the Beast? If you are a boy, which do you want to be like?

3. Do you think the Beast discovered something new about himself the longer he knew the girl? If yes, what thing or things do you think he discovered?

4. What did the Beast eventually decide to do to protect the girl? What did it cost him?

God's Likeness

We can understand some things about ourselves better if we first look at God and learn what He is like. The first few chapters of the Bible tell us how God created man and the universe. When He had finished making the earth, God said, "...Let Us make man in Our image, according to Our likeness" (Gen. 1:26a).

What does this tell us about God? The key words are, "Let Us." They show us why God made us. For example, what would you mean if you said, "Let's go swimming!" Your words would indicate that you wanted to go swimming, right? In a similar way, it's plain from God's words that He *wanted* to make us in His own image.

Thus, the desire to make people like Himself is part of God's nature. That is, God wants to reproduce Himself. He wants children that grow up to be just like He is! He is in the baby business!

Since God made us to be like Him, we too have the desire to reproduce ourselves. He made us to function like Him. He designed us to want to reproduce ourselves. Therefore, our desire to be in the baby business is natural.

This desire to have children is present in both men and women from an early age. It's part of who we are! By the time boys and girls are teenagers, the desire to produce babies has become a very powerful factor that influences their thoughts, their emotions, and their bodies. Yet, the nature of this desire is not the same for boys as it is for girls. Indeed, this powerful desire works in such a *totally different* manner in boys than in girls that it could hardly be more different!

A girl is given a natural desire for a life-long relationship with a man who will love her and defend her no matter what it costs him. This relationship is essential both for her happiness and for the fulfillment of her ability to safely birth and raise children in the likeness of her husband and herself. This desire to marry and have children is very strong in a girl. Because a girl's primary concern is to establish the necessary relationships and conditions to raise children, her very nature seeks a romantic, happy, faithful relationship with the man who is (or will be) the father of her children.

The God-given desire of boys is very different. Sometime between the ages of eight and ten, when girls are beginning to receive visions of the man God will give them to protect them, boys begin to experience unexplainable and embarrassing physical stimulation from pictures and from close physical contact with girls. Their physical bodies are responding with strong sexual responses and desires to the innate desire to reproduce, but their emotional responses lack the female vision or heart's desire for a romantic and faithful relationship. Physical response is it! Boys simply do not look for a meaningful relationship the way girls do.

On the one hand, the desire for a meaningful relationship will later turn out to be one of the things that makes a boy willing to go through fire and kill dragons in order to win the girl he loves! First, however, he must go through fire or he will never be able to sustain a faithful relationship with one woman.

The next few chapters describe what God has built into the nature of men and of women that enables each to establish faithful relationships. Again, remember that God's design for girls is totally different than it is for boys!

Things to Think About

1. Have you ever talked to your parents about their thoughts toward each other before they were married? What do you think your mother wanted most from your father?

2. What do you think your father wanted most from your mother?

3. What differences do you see in what your parents might have wanted or needed from each other?

4. Do you think God has feelings of joy when He has a new child? How does God have children?

The Bonding of Women to Men

We have already seen that God wants us to be like He is. Like Him, He also created us to enjoy and value relationships with others. Marriage is the most significant relationship formed between a man and a woman. Because marriage is filled with struggles and temptations that threaten to destroy it, God has provided for men and women to bond with each other. That is, their souls are so joined that they will always consider the marriage partner to be the most important person in the world.

Thus, bonding provides the glue that helps to hold a marriage together. It is the essential ingredient that provides for contentment within marriage and the cement that encourages both husband and wife to pay any price to work out their problems and remain faithful to each other. When bonding has truly occurred between a man and a woman, they will not be easily persuaded to harm or break the relationship through unfaithfulness or divorce. Indeed, each safeguards the relationship by valuing his or her spouse more highly than other people.

This provision of God shows that He loves us and is working for our good, because bonding encourages us to stay within the boundaries God has provided for right relationships between men

11

and women and to avoid the pain of violating them. If men and women observe these boundaries and follow God's rules, they enjoy the greatest blessings of living under His protection. Bonding therefore occurs naturally as a gift of God to strengthen marriage.

The rule for women is that they will bond with the first man with whom they have sexual intercourse. This is true because a girl's emotions, dreams, and hopes attach to the first boy she gives

**The
Dragon**

herself to completely. She sees in him the one she has been waiting for, her knight in shining armor who will love her and defend her for the rest of her life. From that time on, she will continue to pour out all her love and nurture onto him.

This response is no small matter. All a woman's creativity, the powerful love in her heart to help her man be successful and happy, attaches to this boy. No matter how big a jerk he may be or how he may appear to others, her love covers his weaknesses so that she hardly notices them. (Since most guys are jerks in one way or another, it is really good that God has provided for a woman's love to blind her to his faults and for her soul to be bonded to his in unending faithfulness and dedication!)

It is no wonder, then, that problems arise when a girl does not marry the boy with whom she first has sex. First, the benefit of the natural bonding process is lost because she will never bond the same way with the next boy or boys, and second, her heart will never totally belong to the man she eventually marries because she will continue to think about the first boy for the rest of her life. Even in love-making, when a woman's thoughts should be completely centered on her husband, she will often find herself thinking about that first boy.

How awful! Unhappiness and discontentment await the girl who gives herself to a boy or a man other than her husband. Even if that boy or man mistreats her, she will never be freed from the natural ties that formed when she first gave herself to him. Indeed, she may know that there are better men or better husbands, and she may marry another, but her soul will never bond with that man in the same way.

Great pain and disillusionment also occur when a woman discovers that men do not bond to women in the same way. Because women are so different in this, they find it difficult to understand that *boys don't bond to girls sexually*! What a surprise for a girl who gives herself to her boyfriend to "help" him love her. She winds up bonded to the boy and later discovers that he is not bonded to her at all!

Many girls have been shocked and injured for life because they discovered much too late that boys operate on a completely different wavelength. Although male bonding is different, this doesn't mean that God hasn't provided a way for a man to be joined to his wife so that he will never want to leave her. This is the topic for our next chapter.

Things to Think About

1. At the end of the story *Beauty and the Beast*, do you think the prince could ever leave the girl? Why or why not?

2. If a wife walks out on her husband and gets into a sexual affair with another man, what might this tell you about her background before she married?

5

Male Bonding to Women

L et's look in more detail at the vision God gives to girls. What do they expect their knights in shining armor to do to win them?

Most fairy tales require the hero to fight a dragon, destroy evil, climb a difficult castle wall—or a combination of all three—to win the hand of his true love. Or he might be required to brave fire and water, or even to face death, to rescue his princess. Yes, indeed! Winning the girl never comes cheaply or easily.

In real life, the challenges may not be as exciting or as evident as in fairy tales, yet any young man who would successfully win his beloved must overcome fear and face personal risks to *prove his love for her.* In some way, he must face danger to rescue her and set her free.

Why has God designed things this way? First, a man must discover the true value of a girl in his own heart before he can ever be motivated to die for her. He will not do it willy-nilly. Because a boy does not know his own heart until he is forced to face death or something very close to it, the price to win his beloved must be very high. Only then can he discover what he is willing to endure to safeguard his sweetheart. Once he has made this sacrifice, his

TRUE LOVE   **COURAGE**
FAITHFULNESS   **VISION**

**The character of the Knight in
Shining Armor**

love is securely established, forever. He is bonded. Never again will he doubt whether his girl is worth any price. He knows she is because he faced the danger and paid the price.

Second, a woman needs to be secure in her man's love, to never doubt that he loves her and would do anything to protect her and assure her happiness. An insecure woman is not free. Until she is secure—first in the love of her father, then of her husband— she is not free to love others. Indeed, she cannot truly love them.

God's requirement that men should risk and brave various dangers to win their sweethearts is also essential because boys who never face danger will not grow into men. Until a boy pays a price to win the girl of his dreams, he never really grows up or knows who he is! He remains a boy. Boys require much nurture and they never give girls much security.

When a man is truly bonded to a woman, he will never let her go or throw her away. He has paid too great a price to risk losing her! He is bonded to her for life! This bonding permits both the man and the woman to be secure in their love because *both the man and the woman know the woman's value to the man*! This provides a solid foundation for marriage.

Thus, God's design and purpose provide for the man to become bonded to his girl before the wedding by overcoming the various obstacles that would prevent him from winning her love and her hand in marriage, and for the woman to become bonded to the man on their wedding night when she and her new husband first share the marriage bed in sexual intercourse. Through this godly process, the boy becomes perfected as a man and the girl is perfected as a woman.

Why would a boy die for a girl? Can he do this without actually dying? Of course he can! No bride wants a dead groom! In truth, this mystery of a young man's dying for his bride goes beyond our physical experiences. There is more to it than natural death. It points to wonderful mysteries that are planted in the hearts of all people so we can experience the life and nature of God.

As important as this human bonding between a man and woman is, God's design of boys and girls reveals an even bigger truth because the same giving and receiving of love is necessary between God and man. God loves us, but we are not free until we personally know and believe in His love. Even as the woman must be secure in the love of her beloved, so God's children must be secure in His love. God wants us to know beyond any doubt that He loves us and that we are valuable to Him (see Jn. 3:16)!

Later in this book, we will learn more about the Father's plan to rescue us through our heavenly Bridegroom. Then we will also unveil the mystery of the soul-bonding that must occur between the Bride and the Groom.

Things to Think About

1. Are boys and young men naturally "knights in shining armor," or do they learn to behave this way?

2. Can a girl "make" her knight in shining armor risk death for her?

3. Have you ever liked or loved someone so much you would do anything for him or her? Are such feelings of devotion an accident or do they come from God?

4. If these feelings of loyalty and faithfulness are from God, do you think He might have a good plan to help the desired relationships to happen? If so, what?

6

More About God's Design of People

God designed men and women to do different things. Thus, He built into them differences that go beyond those that are evident in their desires to reproduce themselves and in the process of soul-bonding. Some differences are obvious. Others require more careful thought and examination.

Why, for example, do boys tend to fight a lot? Why do girls talk more about people while boys talk more about things, especially competitive things? Why do women share their feelings more easily than men? These and zillions of other differences in what men and women want, how they think and talk, and what makes life interesting and fulfilling for them can be discovered by those who take the time to look.

Some things require the cooperation of both man and woman for their successful completion. This is particularly evident in the case of reproduction, which we have started to discuss. We must remember, however, that reproduction is more than sex and babies. There is also the matter of *raising up children*. Do you suppose this too will reveal some differences between men and women?

A baby needs two key provisions to survive and mature. First, it must be nurtured (receiving nourishment and healing), and second, it must have security (protection). God has designed the man and the woman to provide these necessities. Yet, they are not equally responsible to provide both components that are necessary for the child's well-being. Instead, God has allocated a primary responsibility to each. He has designed women to provide the child's nurture, and men to provide security.

These needs, though, continue into adulthood. Men, especially, continue to need nurture, and women continue to need security. Thus, grown people still depend on others to provide these necessities. Within the marriage relationship, God has provided for the husband and the wife to receive nurture and security from each other.

Did you know that the first times God describes Himself in the Bible by a name, He reveals Himself as the provider of these two needs? Yes! First, when Abraham was in a scary situation in which he chose to honor God instead of an earthly king, God said to him, "Do not fear, Abram, *I am a shield to you...*" (Gen. 15:1b). So, God first described Himself as a shield, providing security.

Shortly thereafter, when Abraham and Sarah had completely lost hope that they would ever have their own child, God said, "I am *El Shadday* (shad-dah´ee)" (Gen. 17:1), which in English is translated "God Almighty." In Hebrew this name means that God is "all sufficient, able, more than enough breast," as in a woman's breast. Thus, God said that He was sufficient to supply nurture to Abraham's forthcoming son, Isaac, through barren 90-year-old Sarah. God would be the life-giving breast.

Again we see how God has made us to be like Himself. The man is designed to be a shield and the woman a breast. The differences between girls and boys are all related to this.

A girl always needs security. God intends to provide this for her through a man; first her father, then her husband. In the same way, a boy never outgrows his need for nurture. Initially this need is met by his mom; after marriage a man's wife provides his nurture.

Whenever parents do not meet their sons' and daughters' needs, or spouses do not provide for the needs of their mates, personal growth and fulfillment is hindered and may even stop.

Another way to describe God's provisions for men and women is to say that women are breasts not only for their babies but also for their husbands, and men are shields not only for their daughters but also for their wives. Men need the nurture freely given by a loving mother or wife if they are to be content and fulfilled. Women need to be protected by both their fathers and their husbands if they are to be happy, healthy, and secure.

Loss occurs whenever these basic needs of men and women are not met. A woman cannot continually nurture if she does not feel secure within her man's love and provision. Without the security provided by a good man, a woman is easy to destroy. In a similar manner, men, who are designed to provide physical, economic, and emotional security for women, need the nurture of their wives to survive the beating they take in the world. Without a good woman, a man is easy to destroy.

As long as we're protected and nurtured, women and men can do anything! God's provisions make us "bulletproof." Problems develop only when these protective measures established by God are not functioning correctly. Then we are exposed to the assault of the world and damage occurs. This breakdown in function and role led to the downfall of Adam and Eve. In the next chapter we'll see what happened to Adam and Eve—and to us—because of their loss.

Things to Think About

1. Do words in a conversation have the same meaning for a girl as a boy? Why or why not?

2. How does homosexual pairing oppose God's design for natural balance?

21

7

Our Weakness: How Man Fell

Think about the story of Adam and Eve. Who did satan lead astray? Why did he try to fool Eve? Where was Adam when the serpent deceived her? Might Eve have been unprotected when the beguiler came to her? How did Eve respond to satan's attack? What did she in turn do to Adam? What was his response?

From the things we've already talked about, what do you think were Adam and Eve's weaknesses? Go ahead and make a guess! It should not surprise you that satan attacked Adam and Eve through their points of weakness.

The third chapter of Genesis tells us that satan lied to Eve about her happiness. He convinced her that God was holding out on her by refusing to give her everything that was good for her and that she could be like God, knowing good and evil. Eve believed satan and, therefore, disobeyed God by eating the forbidden fruit.

Eve had clear instructions from God. She had to choose whether she would obey or disobey them. I wonder what might have happened had Adam shielded Eve against satan's lies and the invitation that destroyed her life. In any case, Adam did not defend Eve from satan's attack, and Eve, being deceived, chose to go her own way. You know the rest. She died.

Today millions of girls are being deceived in the same way that satan deceived Eve. The father of lies convinces girls that they can achieve happiness by going their own way with no shield of protection. Because girls are suckers for a lie, they are easily deceived and led astray. This ultimately leads to their destruction.

Poor Adam. We don't know why he failed to defend Eve. We only know that a breakdown clearly occurred. The resulting loss was compounded when Adam took the nurture that Eve gave him, the fruit of the forbidden tree, and ate it. He, too, was thus destroyed through his point of weakness, his need to be nurtured by Eve.

The same thing happens today. Boys, who are suckers for receiving nurture from girls, take whatever nurture girls offer, whether or not it is the right nurture. When the nurture they accept is wrong for them, they die.

When Adam and Eve fell, they not only died (became separated from God), they became even more vulnerable in their points of greatest weakness. Today, the greatest weakness of men is their tendency to accept the wrong nurture, and the greatest weakness of women is their inclination to be deceived by going their own way without a shield of protection. Yes, we are selfish, prideful, hateful people who do many things to grieve God, but the characteristics that cause the greatest damage in our lives are primarily the result of the individual weaknesses of men and women. Women are easily deceived. Men take wrong nurture. These are the tendencies that destroy us.

The natural motivation of all men and women, boys and girls, is to resist what God offers us because we believe that He is holding out on us. This increases our vulnerability to deception and wrong nurture because it perverts our perception of our weaknesses and our true needs.

But, God has a rescue plan. The vision of girls and the desire of boys will be satisfied by God's rescue plan.

Things to Think About

1. If you wanted to get one of your parents to believe a lie, who would you choose to try to deceive, your mom or your dad?

2. Have you ever shopped for groceries with your dad when he didn't have a list? How does his shopping compare with your mom's? Why are there differences or similarities?

3. When you go into a convenience store with brothers and sisters, or other girls and boys, who are the most likely ones to buy soda pop, cookies, candy, etc.? Why?

4. Can you think of an area in your life in which giving into sin a first time has given you a greater urge to repeat the sin? Have you found a way to control this desire? If so, how?

8

Comparing Girls and Boys

Girls and boys look nearly the same when they are born. For a while they also act the same, but before long they begin to show big differences in both appearance and behavior. By the time they reach the teenage years, they are vastly different. These differences continue to grow throughout adulthood. By the time men and women grow old, their differences in appearance become less apparent, but their differences in behavior are greater than ever.

We saw earlier that God describes Himself in three ways in the early part of the Bible. First, He reproduces in His likeness. Second, He is a shield. Third, He is a breast. All people, men and women, are created in God's likeness. The distinctions we see between the genders reflect the differences in the design of a shield and a breast. If we examine these two things, it is not hard to see their dissimilarities. Let's see what they are.

First, a shield is not alive. It is an inanimate object—a thing. A breast, on the other hand, is very much alive. It is living and personal. The differences between an inanimate object and a personal, living object form the foundation for nearly all the key differences between the way men and women think and behave, including the way they communicate. Before we look at these discrepancies in greater detail in later chapters, let us examine the fundamental objects that are the basis for these differences.

A shield is used in war. It is not just a limited covering like a roof, clothing, or sunscreen, which provide minimal protection against some but not all things. Instead, a shield is designed to provide maximum protection in the midst of mortal combat.

Mortal combat is no small skirmish. Life is at stake because people are trying to kill you. Swords, arrows, spears, and flaming missiles all smash into the shield, trying to weaken or evade it. A successful shield takes the blows, protecting whoever is behind it, but not without cost. Damage often occurs, damage that must be repaired before another battle.

A breast is very different from a shield. It is used only in the most personal relationships between a woman and her baby or a woman and her husband. Nothing else. It is used for nurturing. Nothing else.

A breast is the part of a woman's body that most represents her nurturing nature. When she becomes pregnant with her husband's seed, her body is totally dedicated to nourishing the baby. After the child is born, this nurturing work is transferred to her breasts. Even the antibodies that protect the baby from disease are given through the mother's milk.

In a similar manner, a woman's breasts are used to nurture her husband. According to the Bible, a wife is her husband's fountain (Prov. 5:18), and he is to be satisfied by her breasts at all times (Prov. 5:19).

A breast is not made for combat. If it is bruised or mistreated, it will stop working. Therefore, it must be protected by a breastplate. The husband is meant to be the breastplate for his wife. The wife is to be the source of all nourishment and healing for her husband, enabling him to remain in the battle to defend and protect her. This is the way God designed men and women to relate to each other and to live in harmony. It is His plan for their protection and well-being.

Placed together in a covenant of marriage, the shield and the breast each give life to the other, though in very different ways. The shield faces outward, providing the physical, economic, and emotional security that guarantees that his wife and family will survive. Meanwhile, the breast focuses her attention inward, strengthening life within the family and nurturing its relationships to encourage the growth and health of the entire household and of each individual member. Together, the shield and the breast equip each other and their children to face the world with security and a sense of personal value.

Things to Think About

1. Do you agree with these descriptions of the shield and the breast as God's intent for men and women? Does this plan fit the girl's vision as it was described in Chapter 1?

2. Who do you think receives the most nurture from sex, the husband or the wife? Why? What might interfere with or destroy this nurturing benefit?

3. How might a woman draw strength and security from having sex with her husband? Why? What might interfere with or destroy this protective benefit?

9

Attributes Given to Boys and Girls

God has given special strengths to men and women to help them carry out their particular work for the well-being of each other and of the family. These unique characteristics are easily seen.

Males naturally have bodies and behavior that are suited for combat. From his earliest days with his friends, a boy likes to confront and contest. He is stronger and faster than a girl, and he responds more quickly to attack. Boys often push and pound on each other for fun, giving little thought to it. Even when they truly fight, boys usually recover quickly with no lasting results.

This is not true for females. They are essentially nonconfrontational, hating conflict and doing much to avoid a quarrel. If a fight occurs, girls carry the bruises for a long time.

Although they are easily injured, women and girls have great power to nurture, to care for others, to restore, to make peace, to create, and to decorate a place of rest and refuge. They excel at preparing food (especially to delight the senses of men or boys) and at giving gifts or other remembrances that delight others. True to their nurturing nature, girls do not get sick as easily as boys, and even when they are sick, girls have more power than boys to help others who are also sick. As long as they are safe and protected, females usually enjoy providing for the needs and enjoyment of others.

All these natural differences between girls and boys go along with the physical differences that begin to be apparent by the age of 11 or 12. These differences make girls and boys attractive to each other. Yes! We really like what we see. Yet, it is not only physical appearance but also behavior that draws males and females together. We feel good when we are close to somebody who has something that we want but don't have ourselves. The very fact of our differences fascinates us and encourages us to seek the company of members of the opposite sex to provide the good things we are missing but need.

Eventually we make the amazing discovery *that we have something that someone else wants. We can make somebody else feel good!* Wow! Do lights ever start to flash in us then! Zowie!! We've never experienced anything like this, and it sure feels great!

We all love to be *increased,* that is to be made greater than we are. Whenever another person comes close to us and shows us that he or she is made *bigger* because of us, our lives are changed forever! We love it! We find a personal value and identity we never had before.

This new sense of identity and value usually begins in the teen years. From then on we play a different ball game as we take notice of those people who make us feel bigger and better because we make them feel bigger and better. In so doing we learn to grow away from ourselves toward others.

This mutual attraction is all part of God's plan. It is His intent. Yet, there is danger here. Our fascination with this new discovery makes us vulnerable to believing a lie and really messing up our lives. This is the time we are very easily entrapped.

Things to Think About

1. Have you yet made the wondrous discovery that you make another person feel really good about himself (or herself)? How does this make you feel?

2. If you build a relationship with another person because he (or she) makes *you* feel good, what becomes most important in the relationship? Do you see a potential problem in this?

3. When does selfishness become a problem? Is this normally a problem for you?

4. What does the Bible say about giving and receiving? (See Acts 20:35.) Can you see how you might be deceived about this with another person who likes you?

10

Sovereignty: Who's the Head?

Boys play king of the mountain from the time they are little. When they start spending time with girls, they continue this practice by teasing them, bossing them, and trying to be their king, too. There is a good reason boys do this. They are following their instincts because God designed them to be the *head* or *shield* over their family. Indeed, God holds a man responsible for both the actions and the well-being of his wife and children. Check it out in the Bible.

When Jezebel, Ahab's wife, murdered Naboth to steal his field for her husband, God held Ahab responsible (1 Kings 21:1-19). When Adam and Abraham made bad decisions because they followed what their wives told them, God held them responsible (Gen. 3:6-19; Gen. 16-17). God also says that He passes iniquity on to children based on what their fathers, not their mothers, have done (Ex. 20:5; Num. 14:18; Deut. 5:9). Men take the heat for all final decisions.

The Scriptures also establish that man is to be the *head* over his family just as Christ is the head of the Church (Eph. 1:22; 5:23). He is responsible to act wisely and to exercise strength and courage to do what is right for the well-being of his wife and children. Both males and females know instinctively that it is right for the man to be the leader and to bear the final responsibility for all decisions in the home.

Therefore, a boy naturally starts the game of conquest from his earliest times with girls, even though his initial efforts may not be sexual. Whenever he gains influence over a girl in any manner— be it over her affections, her priorities, her time, her schedule, her car, her money, her friends, or her phone calls—he begins to rule over her. His behavior then becomes totally different than it was before his conquest. Indeed, he will often act like a little boy, threatening or pouting until he gets his way, if he fails to gain control in a particular area of his girl's life or if he begins to lose power.

Sex is the final seal of sovereignty or headship over a girl. Once affections are exchanged between a boy and a girl, the boy will persist in seeking sex, with or without a marriage covenant. One of the noteworthy dangers in this process is that the girl inherently seeks to nurture the boy, to meet his needs, and to be submissive to his authority over her. Thus, the boy has great power to draw his girl into sexual submission without a marriage covenant. Girls were not designed to resist this kind of pressure. That's why they need the protection of somebody who is stronger than the boy. This is the role of the girl's father.

This male pressure to submit compounded by the female desire to nurture and please is also the reason why it is very tough for a girl to take something back once she has given it to a boy. Anything given to a boy becomes part of his territory. He will go crazy if anything or anyone threatens it or takes it away. Just like a male animal will fight to defend his territory, so a boy will fight to retain ownership over what he considers to be his with a girl. Therefore, once a girl permits a boy to exercise sexual freedom with her, she usually cannot stop him in the future, even if she feels bad about their sexual involvement and wants to stop it.

Like everything else in our lives that is touched by sin, male sovereignty, when it is abused, brings sorrow and heartache. It destroys women instead of fulfilling its God-given responsibility to protect them. Indeed, what God intended for the good of both men and women harms each by stealing part of their natural strength. This is true because males who seduce females fail completely in their God-given responsibilities.

Men or boys who require females to submit to them sexually may not realize at first what they have lost, for they are completely taken with their conquest. In time, however, they will learn what a heavy price they must pay for misusing their God-given authority. First, they will discover that they have destroyed what should be a man's most prized possession: the value and purity of a woman. Second, they will find out that they have thrown away the gifts of manhood that God gave them to use in being successful men. (We'll talk more about this in a later chapter.) God intends that male sovereignty should always be used to guard and protect a woman, never to conquer and destroy her.

Things to Think About

1. How does God's word to Eve in Genesis 3:16 relate to what we learned in this chapter?

2. Do you think some girls try to use sex to gain control over a boy? What might lead a girl to do this? Do you see this in Genesis 3:16?

3. Can sex outside marriage that is the result of letting nature take its course produce happiness for the boy? For the girl?

4. What is happiness to you?

11

Setting the Stage for the Lie

The incredible things that start to happen between guys and girls in the teenage years put most young people to a new test. They are drawn into their first male-female relationships outside the family. Most teenagers find great joy in discovering that they can satisfy the needs and desires of another person. This gives them new identity and value and releases a new power to give. The more young people experience this new joy, identity, value, and power, the more they try to make it happen.

Say, for example, that a girl discovers a boy who makes her feel important, worthwhile, and feminine, even while she brings out his courage, strength, and masculinity. Naturally, they want to do more and more for the other person, which in turn brings more and more good feelings for themselves. Apart from the natural protection set by God for men and women, this natural tendency in each of us to try to get more for ourselves can draw us toward destruction. Let's talk about this.

As we have said, girls think in terms of building strong personal relationships. This is a major factor that makes them vulnerable to believing a big lie. Like Eve, they are easily deceived—and destroyed.

Boys, on the other hand, are basically "brain dead" when it comes to relationships with girls. They are more concerned with how the physical affection of the girl makes them feel than with the relationship it may build. Thus, the girl is thinking on a deeper level than the boy. She is looking beyond the immediate affection to the ultimate goal of building a relationship.

Often the girl perceives that the guy is shallow and she therefore does everything in her power to help him toward a deeper relationship. She does this because a stronger relationship means more security for her and she can then give more without being hurt. Indeed, most girls believe that they can freely and willingly do all the things they were designed to do, if they can just establish the solid, secure relationships they desire and need.

Inevitably, a girl must decide how much she can give to make her guy feel good before her giving makes her feel bad. As the boy pressures her to give more to him physically from her body, the girl wants to make him feel good, but she can't help wondering what will happen to the relationship. If she believes her giving will strengthen the relationship, she often gives more, even if she would prefer not to. Yet, she is somewhat cautious because she does not want to destroy the relationship she already enjoys. This conflict within a girl creates a great dilemma for her. She wants to give because she worries that withholding her body from the boy will hurt him and their relationship, yet she fears that giving too much will destroy her happiness and self-respect.

The girl also experiences pressure to give in to the boy's demands because she enjoys doing things that make him feel good. In essence, she feels good making him feel good. Remember! Girls are not designed to be confrontational. They want to nurture. Thus, a girl's biggest problem is that her heart was designed to do just what the boy wants her to do! She dreams of building the boy up and making him happy. Her vision is to give herself to him freely, to pour out her life on him in every way.

This is God's design for women. How can a young girl possibly resist her desire to be delightful and pleasing to this boy? What defense does she have against messing up her life?

Things to Think About

1. How does God protect girls from the situation described above?

2. What difference might it make if a boy had to make the same claims and promises to a girl's father as he makes to the girl? Could most guys do this?

3. Can a girl's father tell when a boy is lying? Can a girl?

4. Should a girl be required to prove her love to a boy before she marries him? Is this part of the female vision that we spoke of earlier?

12

Believing the Big Lie

When a boy really starts to apply the pressure to have sex, he will tell the girl that he loves her and insist that she trust him. He will also ask her to prove her love for him. Then the girl's thinking starts going something like this: *Maybe he's right! Maybe if I really love him like he says he loves me, I should trust him and give myself to him. Maybe if I do that, he will love me more because he knows I love him. If I risk and entrust this valuable part of myself to him, he will appreciate me and love me more.*

Inevitably the girl's thoughts end up at her desire for commitment and a meaningful relationship: *Maybe if I give myself to him sexually and he becomes assured that I love him, his love for me will grow and I will receive the commitment and security I really need from him!*

The unfortunate part of this thought process is that the girl assumes that boys and girls think and act in the same manner, and that her guy is therefore thinking in the same way she is. She thinks that she needs to prove her love for him like she wants him to prove his love for her. She also expects him to bond to her through sex because that is how she will bond to him. She may also think that *taking the first initiative and being the first to risk and show commitment* are the means by which she can strengthen the relationship and

43

possibly secure marriage with him. But these are all lies, and believing them is believing a very *big lie*!

As we have seen, nothing is farther from the truth. Men and boys do not bond through sex. They do not understand security and commitment in the same way girls and women do. They do not esteem females who are no longer pure because they have given themselves sexually. When a girl believes the *big lie* that the giving of herself sexually will secure the boy's love for her and his commitment to her, the girl, in fact, loses the very thing she seeks. The destruction of her purity ruins her attraction and pushes the boy away. Not having to pay a price for the girl makes her cheap!

Girls, beware! You do not have to prove your love for your guy. All the thoughts that encourage you to give yourself to him sexually as proof of your love for him are lies. You should never have to go first. This is the boy's responsibility. God designed him to prove his love for you and take the risks.

When marriage takes place because a girl and a boy have shared the intimacy of the sexual relationship, there is always guilt and great loss. Added to the guilt of losing her virginity is the girl's discovery that giving herself did not accomplish what she had intended. The girl will never know her husband's true love. Indeed, she *cannot* receive what she so desperately seeks because giving in to a boy's demands does nothing to increase his love for her or her security in his love. She has accomplished nothing by yielding to his persuasion—absolutely nothing! Oh, she may be married to him like she dreamed, but the marriage will not give her the security and love that were part of her vision. He will not be her knight in shining armor, dedicating his life to guard and protect her! Just the opposite will be true. She will lose the value that warrants protection.

Girls are not designed to resist the persuasive arguments of boys. They need to be safeguarded from the foolishness both of the boy and of their own hearts. They need protection to stop them from messing up! Where shall they seek this protection?

Usually a girl's father provides her protective covering. He is the one who helps her to avoid and withstand a boy's pressure. He is the one who requires that the boy be accountable for the girl, passing through fire and giving a heavy soul-price for her so that he is bonded to her for life. Then the boy may marry her. Then he may have her completely—that is, sexually and in every other way. By then his love for her will be certain and she can pour out her love upon him for life.

Remember, a girl's vision can be fulfilled only when she is not taken in by the *big lie*! If a girl's father will not or cannot provide a protective covering for her, the girl must seek it elsewhere, for without that covering her chances of happiness are severely lessened. A girl cannot secure the love and commitment of a boy by taking the risk and giving herself to him. The risk is the boy's to take. The proof of love is his to give. Then the vision of the girl, held close in her heart from her early years, may be accomplished, giving her the love and security she needs.

Things to Think About

1. What shows a girl her true value? Can she accomplish this by giving herself to a boy?

2. How does a boy's willingness to deny himself and wait for her show the girl her true value?

3. Why might a boy know fear in facing a girl's father? Is this good or bad? Is this question also related to the value of the girl?

4. Who has God charged with the responsibility to cherish and protect a girl's true value? Why? Who else might provide this protection if this person cannot or will not guard and defend her?

13

Fruit of the Big Lie

There is a spirit that bears bitter fruit when a girl believes *the lie*. What do you think this spirit is?

Think for a moment about the thoughts that go through a girl's head as she tries to decide whether or not she should yield to the boy's desires. (See the first three paragraphs of the last chapter.) What is she essentially deciding? Let's take a closer look.

The girl's thoughts are basically this: *If I give in, maybe I'll get what I need from him: deeper security in our relationship.* Thus, *the lie* is not readily apparent because it is camouflaged in words like "proving my love," "building relationship," and "making him happy." Yet, it is present, because the girl's thoughts boil down to this: *If I give my body to this guy, maybe I'll get the commitment I need from him to meet **my** need, to provide for **my** security.*

Now take a good hard look at this proposition, for that is what it is. It's a proposition—a sexual proposition. It's the proposition of harlotry or prostitution.

The basic trade in all prostitution is a female giving sex in order to get something from a male to strengthen her security.

This often degenerates all the way to a man paying money for sex and a woman paying sex for money, but other forms of degradation also result along the way. Harlotry will also pass on into marriage, such as when a woman withholds herself from her husband to get him to prove his love, to do a particular job, or to change his behavior. Giving sex as a *reward* for good behavior or for doing something well is also a face of harlotry.

All this is prostitution. It destroys a woman's security and devours a man's manhood. The woman becomes entrapped, losing the freedom within the relationship that she sought. Often she hates herself for using sex to get what she wants. The man, in turn, feels robbed. He, too, hates what the sexual relationship has become, but he is helpless to correct it.

God intends for sex to be used in one way only: For a husband and wife to give to each other freely to satisfy each other's needs, to build up the relationship, and to produce godly seed. Then sex is a wonderful gift.

Sex used in trade is always harlotry. Harlotry is always abusive and destructive. *It causes a woman to view exchanging her body for something she wants or desires as the expected norm.* Sadly, she never truly receives what she needs. She remains insecure and unsatisfied. Her original vision from her girlhood becomes warped and unrecognizable. Her romantic desires are not satisfied by her husband. Again and again she relives her original sexual delusions, trying to gain love by giving sex.[1]

Harlotry destroys a woman's chances of being happy. If she leaves her man to secure happiness with another, she will not bond to her next husband if she marries, or to the next man or men she gives herself to. No man can meet her security needs or her other expectations because the marriage or relationship is based on

---

1. Ezekiel, chapters 16 and 23, and Hosea, chapters 1 and 2, reveal how the spirit of harlotry thinks and behaves. See also Psalm 106:35-39.

harlotry. The sale of her body is the foundation of the relationship, instead of the knowledge that she is loved.

Harlotry also destroys men and ruins children. This is true because a woman becomes frigid to her husband, but open to other men. Lacking the bond with her husband that God intends within marriage, the woman will easily leave him. According to the Bible, harlotry is also the only thing that will cause a woman to give up (sacrifice) her children to follow her lusts (see Ezek. 16; 23; Hos. 1–2; Ps. 106:35-39). Whether or not a harlot stays with her children, they suffer because the family unit is broken.

No one in her right mind would open herself to such a spirit and such bitter fruit. Yet it is happening now in our land. *Every day girls and women are deceived into thinking that they can get something they need from their lovers if they give sex.* They believe the *big lie*! Like Eve, they fear that they will miss the best God has for them. Or they are afraid that they will lose their guys. Therefore, they repeat Eve's mistake: They try to get what they want by going their own way and scorning the protection God planned for them to enjoy.

God has a much better way. He takes the risks and gives Himself first, winning our hearts and marrying us after our security has been established. The story of Boaz and Ruth exemplifies this kind of love.

Things to Think About

1. How is a girl's "proving" her love for a boy by sleeping with him harlotry? What is she really proving?

2. How does harlotry damage a boy?

14

Boaz: A Man's Man

God can raise up real men who will treat women right. He can raise up women who will bring out the best in a man, even if the woman has been married before. The key to the success of men and women within their individual roles and within the marriage relationship is following God's plan for men and women. The story of Boaz and Ruth teaches us much about this plan.

Ruth was a widow who left her country to come to Israel to live with her mother-in-law, Naomi. Although Ruth was a foreigner, she had learned to love and trust the God of Naomi, the God of Israel, the true and living God of the Bible. Therefore, she entrusted her life to His keeping by leaving her people and going with Naomi to her dead husband's people.

Now Naomi and Ruth were poor. To provide their food, Ruth went out and began to gather the grain left in the fields by the reapers. By *coincidence*, Ruth happened to go the very first day to a field that was owned by Boaz, a very rich man. Just imagine the thoughts of the young men as they saw Ruth in the field that day. You know and I know what they were thinking!

But this was not the reaction of Boaz to Ruth's presence. If you are a girl who knows God's promises for you, you probably know what Boaz did. As soon as he found out who she was, he ordered his men *not to touch her* and he told Ruth to stay in his fields with his maids and not to go to other fields to glean. Thus, Boaz gave Ruth *physical protection*.

After lunch that day, Boaz did something else for Ruth. He told his men to leave extra grain for her to gather so that when Ruth went home that evening she had an ephah (about half a bushel) of grain. Thus, Boaz also gave Ruth *economic protection* by sending her home with enough grain to sell to help meet her other needs!

In those days, there was a legal provision for widows with no sons that allowed a kinsman-redeemer (a close male relative) to purchase back land that had been lost through death or hardship and to sleep (have sex) with the widow to produce a son who would carry on the family name. When Naomi discovered that Ruth had been working in the field of Boaz, a close relative who could act as a kinsman-redeemer for them, she tried to entice Boaz to sleep with Ruth and take on the responsibility of providing a son to be raised as their heir. Therefore, she told Ruth to bathe, to dress in her prettiest clothes, to put on her best perfume, to go down in the middle of the night to the workplace where Boaz was sleeping, and to sleep at his feet!

When Boaz awoke in the middle of the night and discovered Ruth at his feet, he did something much better than Naomi had expected. Though he was greatly flattered by Ruth's request that he "place his blanket over her" since he was a kinsman-redeemer, Boaz chose not to take advantage of the situation. Instead, he promised to offer Ruth to a kinsman-redeemer who, under the law, was more closely related to Ruth than Boaz was. Then, if the other man would not fulfill his responsibility as kinsman-redeemer, Boaz promised to do so himself.

Boaz promised Ruth something better than she asked of him. He had evidently thought through her situation and knew of the closer relative. He also was prepared to do what was best for her. Why? He had probably fallen in love with her. Boaz's willingness to do his best for Ruth most likely also came from his desire to please God by doing what was right in His sight. If you read the short Book of Ruth (four chapters), you will discover that Boaz loved God dearly. He obviously had God at the center of his life. Therefore, he was willing to submit to God's authority and to trust Him.

Boaz's actions are clearly honorable. Although he was a rich man who could buy anything he wanted, he did not take advantage of Ruth's need when she—a beautiful, desirable woman—came to him in the middle of the night and offered herself to him. Many men would have taken the pleasure she offered. They would not have denied themselves.

Boaz's decision not to accept Ruth's proposal is also noteworthy for another reason. Not only did he resist the invitation of the moment, but by saying "no" he knew that he had probably lost the chance to ever have her. Wow! Is that tough or not? Truth is not only stranger than fiction, it is much better!

Boaz's concern for Ruth is also evident in his next words and actions. First he tells her to sleep at his feet until near dawn; then he sneaks her out of the workplace so that no one will know that she was there! Do you see Boaz's concern not only for Ruth's physical safety but also for her *emotional security*? He didn't want any talk to tarnish her reputation, so he provided a way of escape for her.

The next part of the story is the hardest to understand. What great pain and fire Boaz went through for Ruth. He had already cared for her physical safety, her economic security, and her emotional protection. He had also given her up sexually to do right by her. What a high price to pay! Although he loved her, he would not grasp for what he wanted. Instead, he submitted to God's authority to find out God's will for him and for Ruth.

53

How hard it must have been for Boaz to go to the city gates that day. He probably expected to lose Ruth, but he was still willing to submit to the authorities in a decision over which he had no control. Thus, he offered the man who was a closer relative to Ruth the opportunity to buy Naomi's land and to take Ruth as a wife so that a son might be born and raised to continue Ruth's dead husband's name and the family's ownership of the land.

The man wanted the land, but he didn't want to spend his inheritance on a son who would not bear his name. Therefore, he refused to redeem Ruth, and Boaz got her! Boaz married Ruth and raised a son who bore the name of her deceased husband. The child turned out to be the grandfather of King David.

Boaz's story has been recorded for eternity in the Bible! His willingness to submit to God's authority and to do the right thing for Ruth has earned him a place in history. What can we learn from this story?

- The man must give himself up first and pay a substantial price for the girl.

- The man is responsible to provide physical, economic, and emotional protection.

- The man must deny himself from having sex with the girl until they marry, even though he loves her (and even if she was previously married).

- The man must submit to higher authority and trust God for the results.

- God honors the man who pays the price to do right by his woman.

- God honors the girl who entrusts her life to Him and stays under the protective authority He provides (even if that authority is a woman!).

God has marvelous ways of honoring those who honor Him! He is so wonderful and so good to those who obey Him! He knows the price men pay to be faithful to His plan. He sees the desire of brides to know they are loved. The mysteries of the Book of Ruth confirm God's goodness and providence. They show the principles of God's plan not only for relationships between men and women but also for the relationship between God and His people.

God never asks of us anything that He has not already done for us. He does not ask us to risk anything beyond what He has been willing to do Himself. Everything Boaz did for Ruth, Jesus did for us when He came to be our Bridegroom. Those who submit to His protection will discover true happiness.

Things to Think About

1. Might the story of Ruth and Boaz make a good movie? What true principles does it illustrate?

2. Do you see any similarities between this story and *Beauty and the Beast*? What are they?

3. Can you see how the principles illustrated in this story, in which the man goes first and pays the price for the woman, are confirmed in the history of Jesus Christ and His Bride?

15

Boys: Setting the Stage for the Lie

W hat happens to boys when they are drawn into the *big lie*? Do they get off free? No! They sure don't! Before we examine the price boys pay for believing the lie, let's see what the liar says to them.

The basic need of a boy is nurture. As he grows up, a boy learns that his mother is the primary provider of those things that satisfy his flesh. By the time he reaches puberty, he is used to eating and drinking whenever he wants—which is nearly all the time. He has also discovered the pleasures of music, amusement parks, video entertainment, and other forms of recreation. Again, a boy's mom is often the provider of these diversions, and she rarely says no. Sexual maturity occurs around the age of 12 or 13, and masturbation follows that. It satisfies. But mom is not part of this picture. Neither is dad, in most families. A "secret place" then usually develops in the boy.

As we said in an earlier chapter, the desire to reproduce comes out in a boy as a strong desire to *plant his seed*, to have sex. This nature of a boy leads to sexual excitement that is hard to control. Although this desire for sex may be satisfied by wet dreams, it can easily lead to masturbation and a boy's playing with himself, which causes guilt. Thus, a boy usually keeps his sexual play secret, or he shares it with only a few. The stage is now set for relationships with girls and the *big lie*. A boy also has a natural desire to have authority over a girl. Although this desire to be the head is perverted, it is still part of God's order and is built into his genes. Sexual possession is a seal of this headship.[1]

This desire to exercise authority is one of the things behind the "king of the mountain" instinct that becomes evident in young boys. They don't see the risk in the games they have played all their lives to satisfy this desire to win and to be on top. In a similar manner, boys see little risk in having sex.

Remember, a boy's desire to have sex is not related to creating a strong, secure relationship with a girl. Unlike a girl, he doesn't view having sex as a security issue at all, as long as he's not exposed and embarrassed. That's the only risk. His flesh sees it only as a nurture issue and a headship issue. All his instincts for adventure, risk, and winning, and his God-given sense of doing something great, now come into play with a girl. Remember, this is all happening in a boy, not a true man.

A boy must go through fire for a girl to become a real man. He may pretend that he is willing to pay a real price for a girl, but most boys are not. They will pretend with their girls, but not with the girls' fathers. Why? Because fathers can't be fooled as easily as girls can. They know the thoughts and desires of boys because they have been there. Fathers are God's gift for girls, given to protect them from boys who are playing games and don't want to be exposed.

What are these games of teenage boys? A boy who has gone through puberty feels desire for a girl and starts to figure out how he can satisfy his need. He likes being with girls, particularly a girl who makes him feel *increased* and able to do good things. Physically touching a girl excites him. Yet, he is never satisfied. He

---

1. Read more about this in Chapter 10, "Sovereignty: Who's the Head?"

always wants more. Indeed, he will take everything he can get that's free, that requires no *real price* to attain it. In other words, he'll be the head if he can get there without paying a price!

In addition to his physical desire, a boy may also have real affection or emotional love for a girl. This introduces another problem because the boy will try to keep his bad character from being exposed to the girl so that she won't think poorly of him. This is usually how a boy becomes entangled in the *big lie*.

Things to Think About

1. How can a boy try to keep a girl from thinking poorly of him when he wants to have sex with her?

2. Will the girl believe the boy? How can she be protected from the boy's intentions?

3. What is the difference between emotional love and real love?

16

Boys: Believing the Big Lie

As boys and girls pass through adolescence, they are confronted by issues that are at the very center of life. *The desire to reproduce that God has placed in them leads to situations of great power and deception.* Both are eager to meet their *own* needs, but their needs are very different. A girl wants relationship, commitment, security, and the fulfillment of her vision of a knight in shining armor carrying her off into the sunset. A boy wants sovereignty and sex.

A boy's desire for sovereignty and sex is compounded by his need to look right to the girl. Therefore, he tries to justify to her what he wants from her. It's even better if he can believe what he wants her to believe!

A boy's desire to get what he wants for himself is also impacted by his moral responsibility. According to God's plan and His ordering in male-female relationships, male headship includes accountability for the success or failure of the relationship. Hence, a guy has a much more powerful need to make things "right" so that he will not feel guilty. Meanwhile, a girl knows in her heart what is right and wrong, but *she also has a sense that the boy should bear the ultimate responsibility for what happens between them.* This is a natural part of her expectation that the boy will provide for her security.

God's plan for men and women is imprinted on the conscience of every boy. Therefore, the boy senses that his love for the girl is the key to making things come out right. Indeed, the only thing that will satisfy everything for both him and his beloved is his proof of true love. The girl also knows this.

Hence, the boy is faced with a choice between God's plan and satan's plan! This is the focal point around which both the *truth* and the *lie* are centered. This is the key. *Yes! The man's **love** for the girl and his responsibility for proving it are at the very center of the male-female relationship.* This love and proof of love are also central to God's pattern in creation and His plan for redemption.

God's design brings us to the issue of love. Love establishes both the security and freedom of the bride. This is the key to her happiness. Therefore, satan tries to pervert *love* and *the proof of love*: the twin pillars of marriage. God loves and risks first to prove His love through the Bridegroom. But satan misrepresents God's plan by trying to force the girl to be the first to risk.

Every boy must face this perversion. It sets before him a terrible dilemma: He knows that the girl needs the security of knowing that he loves her. Therefore, he must honestly assess whether he really does love her. Meanwhile, he wants what he wants. Consequently, he'll move ahead—if he can—before he knows the true answer. Instead of waiting to determine and prove whether he truly loves the girl, he tries to persuade her to have sex now. Sex without real commitment looks like a good deal for him!

Thus, his thoughts go something like this: *Perhaps I can claim that I love her and prove it later on. Who knows? I really may love her. In any case, sex before I prove my love is worth a try. Maybe I can get by with just **saying** that I love her! If I at least say the words, I'll be more acceptable in her eyes. Perhaps then she'll give me more of what I want!* This often works because *girls want to believe that their guys love them.*

Some boys have principles against lying. This kind of guy will try to mislead his girl without actually saying that he loves her. This may involve doing nice things for her, taking her to nice places, and spending money on her. The object is to imply love without actually saying it. Then—if it is convenient later on—without offending his conscience, he can deny that he ever *said* that he loved her. So goes the deception that a boy *thinks* this makes him look more honest.

Unfortunately, many girls will accept this evidence as proof of her guy's love. In truth, it is not, because the girl will be pressured to pay for these nice things with return gifts from her body.

Do you see how the boy has walked into the *big lie?* He has already begun to bargain for the girl's favors by offering her what she wants in exchange for what he wants. This leads to harlotry in the boy. He's paying for sex with promises and gifts that have nothing to do with true love. (Remember: True love from a man is giving himself up to rescue and protect his girl.) He's saying or implying love to persuade the girl to prove her love!

Isn't this the way boys act? They use the method of pressuring or accusing the other person as the best way of turning attention away from their own problems and shortcomings. Many girls with no protection fall for this.

Sometimes boys are conned into thinking that all their great feelings about a girl are really love when they are not. Girls also suffer from this illusion. They cannot discern the truth without actual proof of love by the boy—that's why it's so important! When, however, a boy *pretends* to love a girl, or he says and does what he thinks she wants to hear and receive, he too has been seduced by the father of lies and has begun to walk in harlotry.

All this pretending, deceiving, and bargaining for a girl's body lead to destruction. It's not part of the girl's vision, nor is it part of the gospel of Jesus Christ. No girl ever needs to prove her love for her knight or bridegroom before marriage. This is never within God's will and plan!

Things to Think About

1. Read Proverbs chapter 5. What happens to an immoral boy?

17

More Fruit of the Lie

We asked in the last chapter, What does harlotry do to boys? Do they get off free? No! Although it may appear at first that they do, boys don't get off free when they engage in harlotry. It's true that a boy doesn't bond to a girl through sex—so there's little pain at first when a sexual relationship is broken—but a much worse thing happens. Actually, a boy is killed when he commits sexual immorality. *He loses what God gave him to guarantee his success as a man.* Let's explain.

The Bible indicates in Proverbs chapter 5 that there are three things involved in a man's success. They are strength, vigor (vitality of mind and body), and earning power. Strength is needed to defend and protect and for courage. Vigor is required to find wisdom and to grow. Earning power is necessary to meet his responsibility to provide economic protection. A man can't provide for a family without these three things.

The Bible also declares that a boy loses these essential ingredients of successful manhood when he has sex outside marriage (Prov. 5:9-10). Hence, although a boy may grow up to look like a man on the outside, on the inside he is incapable of fulfilling a man's responsibilities. He's been tricked by the father of lies. Deep inside a *lie* has stolen his manhood.

A man's gifts are given by God to protect women and to support his family. They are directly connected to his reproductive power. Hence, the strength, vigor, and hard-earned goods that are the basis for his success as a man are tied to his seed. If he wastes his seed by misusing the sexual relationship between a man and a woman, it is as if he has poured his seed out on the ground. Like a glass of water that is poured away, his seed and gifts lose their life-giving ability and, thus, are wasted. The Bible says that his manhood is poured out like "streams of water in the street" (Prov. 5:16).

Another way to look at the result of male harlotry is to see that a man's ability to protect women is nullified when he misuses his strength and vigor by having sex outside marriage. Instead of protecting women, he destroys them. Hence, his evil misuse of strength and vigor gives satan the legal authority to steal them. Satan's deception becomes legal because the man has violated God's laws concerning the use of his seed and gifts.

Look around you at all the destroyed marriages: wives with no husbands, kids with no dads, mothers with the sole responsibility of providing for their families—whether by working or by accepting welfare—because their men have failed them. Where has all the money gone? It has been consumed by harlotry. All the man's hard-earned goods have been taken by other men, just like Proverbs 5:10 says. (Read Proverbs 5:1-11.)

How many men do you see who can't hold a job or keep a family, who are constantly losing out, who are always frustrated and ineffective? Their strength and vigor have vanished. They are no longer the head of their homes. You can bet for sure that sexual immorality lies behind their failure. In nearly all the marriages that fail (over 95%), the husband, the wife, or both had sex before marriage.

So the boy's basic desire to reproduce and his motivation to do *something great* have been misdirected through the big lie to produce death in him and in the girl. *At the moment of truth, the boy knew that the issue was **love** and the **proof of love**, but he went the wrong way.*

Boys are not solely responsible for this loss. Many girls have drawn them away from real love and the proof of love by believing the lie that produces death—in them and in the marriage. Until Jesus comes into their lives, things gets rapidly worse. Nothing can stop the progress of death except the *truth and power of life in Jesus Christ.*

Things to Think About

1. What does the Bible say happens when two people agree to sin? Can you think of some biblical examples? (Hint: Read the story of Rebekah and Jacob in Genesis, chapters 27 and 28, or the story of Jonathan and David in First Samuel, chapters 20 and 31.)

2. What should the boy do to prove his love to the girl and at the same time demonstrate that his love is real love, not emotional love?

3. What happens to a girl's vision after she has engaged in immoral sexual intercourse? What has been destroyed?

The Destruction of Men and Women

Part One

The Bible says that a married woman is the chief life-giver for her husband when she has sex with him (Prov. 5:15-19). Why do I say it this way? What about the unmarried woman or the unmarried man? What does sex bring to them?

Sex in marriage is a great gift of God. It enables both the husband and the wife to satisfy their God-given desires to reproduce godly seed in the likeness of God. It also nurtures the man and brings him to godly contentment. Bringing intimate, loving satisfaction to her husband is the woman's gift. In so doing, she too finds godly contentment as she enjoys both his satisfaction and her own. If she gets pregnant, she is secure.

For an unmarried woman, an adulteress or harlot, the Bible says the opposite is true (Prov. 2:16-19; 5:5; 6:24-35; 7:6-27). Instead of giving the man life through the sexual relationship, she brings him death. As we saw in the last chapter, men are destroyed by immorality.

Men were designed by God to protect women physically, economically, and emotionally. Sex outside marriage provides none of these. Indeed, the man opens the woman to devastating risks by having sex with her before he provides for her through the protection of the marriage covenant.

Girls, if you are unmarried, ask yourself the following questions:

- What are the *physical* risks of sex? Suppose you get pregnant. Will you have an abortion or give birth to the baby? How will either choice affect your life? Will your baby be healthy? What about your own health?

- What are the *economic* risks of sex? Who will support you and your baby? Will the boy? Will your parents? Will you? What kind of future awaits you in any of these cases?

- What are the *emotional* risks of sex? What will your parents think? Does the boy really love you? How can you be sure? Will he marry you? If so, can you trust him? What are his priorities? What if he leaves you? What might the future hold for you if the marriage is loveless or broken?

Girls, listen! God did not design you to confront these questions! He created you to be protected from these by a boy who loves you! God knows that you need this protection. He also knows that a boy must invest his soul and pay a high personal price before he can understand the value of a girl. *Male love is proven when the man protects you.* By giving you protection, the man acknowledges that you are worth whatever he has to pay for you. You need the security of his love to nurture him and to bear his children. A life-long marriage covenant that provides protection for a woman and her children is God's intention.

If a boy can't deny himself sex to protect you, then he can't protect you. Where then is your security? You will take it over yourself! Your knight is dead! The vision you received as a little girl is smashed to pieces!

Yes, a girl is destroyed when she discovers how little value she holds in the eyes of her lover. She is destroyed when she learns how weak and undependable he is. This is only the beginning of the destruction that enters her life. A woman who is destroyed by her husband's inability to protect her loses her freedom and her womanhood. She also loses her trust in men and in God. Indeed, *this woman becomes a slave to insecurity. No security will ever be enough.*

Girls, the questions I asked you to consider earlier are only the first problems you will encounter when you have sex outside the protection of marriage. Difficulties in your relationship with your baby and the father of your baby often arise. You may become infected by venereal disease or AIDS and suffer the resulting bitterness and sterility that follow such diseases. Even if you do not become pregnant, lies, broken relationships, and the effects of fear, guilt, and birth control will affect you for the rest of your life.

In addition, once a sinful pattern of sexual intercourse is begun, it is nearly impossible to break. It only leads to more desperation, destruction, and degradation, as a girl begins to see sex as a method to get a boy to bring her happiness. *Then she becomes a slave to insecurity. Whether she is married or single, her appetite will never be satisfied.* Think carefully before you begin this pattern.

Things to Think About

1. How does an insecure woman behave? What does she lust for?

2. What might heal the deep insecurity of a woman who has been destroyed by a man?

19

The Destruction of Men and Women

Part Two

Do you see how a man who is tricked into having a girl sexually outside of marriage destroys her instead of protecting her? He does the opposite of what he's supposed to do! At the same time, harlotry destroys him as well.[1] He grows deeper into his habit, making his need for sex the most important thing in his life. Yet, he is never satisfied. His "needs" get worse and worse until he needs something more exciting.

If a boy did not enjoy pornography before he gave away his virginity, he most certainly will seek it afterward. This is what satan wants. Satan doesn't want the young man to be satisfied because then he can draw him into deeper lusts, driving girls into deeper and deeper futility to satisfy him. In time, the boy will move on to sodomy and other extreme forms of sexual perversion *until he becomes a slave of sensual lusts. Sex, and even perverted sex, will never be enough.*

How does this affect women? Don't they want men who will be satisfied with them? Why would a woman help a man to become

---

1. Read the first nine chapters of the Book of Proverbs to learn how a woman's immorality causes the death of a man.

so perverted that he can never be satisfied? This, too, is a result of believing the *big lie*. Both the man and the woman have been deceived. Because they both agreed to steal what they wanted for themselves, everything turns to dust. That is the way of sin.

Why would a girl want to rob a boy of manhood, especially a boy she might marry? Does she not understand that this turns him into a wimp? Unfortunately, too many girls do not appreciate the impact of sexual immorality on a man. Too late a girl discovers that she has a guy who does not know what is valuable in his life, who is afraid to stand up for her. Too late she understands that she has contributed to his failure by having sex with him before they marry. Does she think she has not been warned? The Scriptures bear abundant witness to the destruction that follows sex outside marriage. Listen to the warnings to the boy:

Suddenly he follows her, as an ox goes to the slaughter, or as one in fetters to the discipline of a fool, until an arrow pierces through his liver; as a bird hastens to the snare, so he does not know that it will cost him his life (Proverbs 7:22-23).

King Solomon had more wives (700) and concubines (300) than any other man. He knew about sex. God also gave him a special gift of wisdom. Thus, he also knew the problems related to sexual misconduct! The first nine chapters of the Book of Proverbs contain his words concerning wisdom and destruction. The instructions boil down to only two topics: (a)methods for seeking wisdom from God and men, and (b) warnings to young men against sexual immorality. Can you see the direct relationship between the two?

Look at the millions of men in our country in their 20s, 30s, and 40s who have thrown their manhood out on the ground like sewage and are now in poverty. They have no character, no families, no jobs, no goods. Indeed, they can't be trusted with anything. They are paying the price for abusing God's good gift of sex. They are being held responsible for their sexual immorality. Yet, they are not alone, for each of these men had a woman who believed the big lie. They, too, are paying a terrible price.

Things to Think About

1. Does the phrase, "each of us has turned to his own way" sound familiar? Where does it come from? How does it describe the deception teens can fall into by believing the big lie?

2. Look up Isaiah 53:6 in a Bible. What is the common problem shared by all people? What solution is offered? Read also Isaiah 53:1. What does this verse say is the key issue of Isaiah chapter 53? Of the Bible? Of this book? Do you really believe this?

3. Isaiah 53 was written more than 700 years before the birth of Jesus Christ. How did Isaiah know these things?

20

Role Reversal

S in always causes death. Whenever two people sin together, the relationship between them dies. The Bible contains many, many examples of this.

Rebekah and her favorite son, Jacob, conspired to lie to Rebekah's husband, Isaac, and steal from Esau, Jacob's brother, the blessing Isaac intended to give to Esau. At first the lie appeared to work, but it ruined Rebekah's relationship with her son. Jacob and Rebekah never saw each other after Jacob fled from home to avoid the anger of his brother. (See Genesis, chapters 28 and 29.)

David and his friend Jonathan loved each other as brothers. When they did right and spoke the truth, God did wonderful things for and with them (see 1 Sam. 19); but when David talked Jonathan into lying to his father, King Saul, they experienced terrible problems. Not only did King Saul know right away that Jonathan was lying (fathers are like this!), but the treachery of David and Jonathan ruined their fellowship. They met only once more before Jonathan was killed.

These stories and many more show that sin ruins relationships. Sometimes the death is instant. Other times it is slow and lingering. The effects of sin between marriage partners is especially painful.

When a man and a woman have pre-marital sex, the death of their relationship begins before the marriage even occurs. Even if they marry, their happiness is doomed and they will endure countless years of slow, agonizing pain. Here's why.

One thing that occurs in a relationship that is dying because of sexual immorality is the reversal of roles. That is, everything becomes backward. The woman becomes the head over the man. When a woman rules over a man, he has to earn his love. Like Samson, who was ruled by his wife Delilah, the reversal of headship may lead to the man's death.

If you read the story of Samson, you will see that he refused to listen to his parents and he went after women "that looked good" to him. When he had sex with a woman, she became the dominant partner in the relationship. Samson's first wife enticed him to reveal a secret that cost him much money. Then one of his best friends took her! Later, Samson fell in love with a woman named Delilah who did the same thing to him when she persuaded him to reveal the secret of his strength. Delilah's treachery cost Samson his life. (See Judges, chapters 14 to 16.) Both women harmed Samson because they had control over him.

The story of David and Bathsheba is another example where sexual immorality led to the headship of the woman and the destruction of the relationship. Bathsheba was the wife of Uriah, but David took her for sex. When Bathsheba became pregnant, David sent for her husband and tried to persuade him to sleep with her so that David's sin would not be revealed. Uriah, being a conscientious soldier, would not enjoy pleasure with his wife while his comrades were in danger. Thus, David instructed Joab, one of his generals, to place Uriah on the front lines where he was killed. Then David took Bathsheba as his wife (2 Sam. 11–12).

David's sexual immorality cost him much. First, you will discover if you read all the stories of the relationship between David and Bathsheba that Bathsheba had control over David. This is particularly revealed in her success in persuading David to make her son Solomon king even though he was not the next one in line for the throne (1 Kings 1; 2:22). Second, David lost his friendship with Joab. When Joab gave David good advice, David wouldn't listen to it. When David gave Joab orders, Joab wouldn't obey! Indeed, Joab killed David's son Absalom in direct violation of David's orders (2 Sam. 18:5,9-15). David was so powerless against Joab that his only solution was to have Solomon kill him after David had died (1 Kings 2:5,28-35).

With the widespread sexual immorality in our society, it should not surprise us that many men are under their wives. The reason is obvious. Instead of following God's plan, men have believed the big lie and have followed satan's plan for the destruction of marriage and of godly seed. They have robbed themselves of happiness by attempting to steal it from girls who were not under protection. Then they married. Now they are reaping the pain of their folly.

Boys, if you want to give up your manhood and place your wife in charge of you, just have sex with her before marriage. You will do both (and more) by making this one big mistake. Girls, if you want to be insecure and anxious, if you want to be unable to trust your husband, if you want to keep him under your thumb, or if you want to be primarily responsible for the welfare of your family, just have sex with your man before you marry him. You will have all this and more. Sexual immorality is the primary cause of marital dysfunction and unhappiness.

Things to Think About

1. What hope might there be for all the people who have already messed up?

2. Do you see the patterns of "self-firstness" at work in you and your family? What happens when this tendency is not controlled?

21

Strongholds

When a worm or a snake bores a hole, he either lives in it or leaves it behind. When water cuts a trench in the ground, the trench remains even after the water is dried up. The same is true of sin. Even as a snake returns to the same hole or water finds the trench it had previously formed, so sin recurs more easily after the first fall.

The Bible says: "...you are slaves of the one whom you obey..." (Rom. 6:16). Therefore, when satan, the enemy, gets you to believe the lie and obey him, you become his slave. In other words, he returns to the same hole or trench that he had built before. He builds a *stronghold* in you.

What is a *stronghold*? Strongholds are of two types: good and bad. Good strongholds are God's gifts for our safety. In fact, God calls Himself our Stronghold or Fortress (Ps. 91:2). Other strongholds are built by those who oppose God. They block God's activity in us and on our behalf.

Those who seek safety with God are expressing their trust in Him. Unfortunately, we are more likely to seek safety in the things we build through our own hands. This is an expression of our lack of trust in God. Such strongholds are the work of satan. He builds them brick by brick as he convinces us to believe his lies. Satan intends that these strongholds built upon lies will keep God out of our lives.

The apostle Paul speaks in Second Corinthians of these strongholds of the enemy (2 Cor. 10:4-6). They are fortresses that house the enemy and protect his lies. Their walls, built of false-hoods and lies, protect and defend evil, even as they try to keep out the truth. The city of Jericho, which Joshua captured after God made the walls fall down, is an example of a manmade stronghold. The strength of Jericho was built on lies, but the lies could not keep out the truth.

One of the lies the people inside Jericho believed was that they were safe inside the walls. In truth, the walls entrapped them and led to their death. Only Rahab, who believed God and trusted Him instead of the walls of Jericho, and her family survived the destruction of Jericho. For Rahab, the destruction of the strong-hold brought about her deliverance into freedom. She changed from the life of a prostitute to that of a godly wife and mother. Her son, Boaz, was one of the most godly men in the Bible. (See Chapter 14 for a description of Boaz's character.) Rahab's deliverance and transformation occurred because she traded the lies of the enemy for the *truth* of God by trusting Him instead of her man-made stronghold.

When satan builds strongholds within us, we too must be freed by the truth of God or we will continue to be held captive by satan's lies. Role reversal is only one of the tragic results for those who choose to have sex outside the marriage covenant. The walls of satan's strongholds continue to get higher and stronger until the marriage is ripped apart—sometimes after 20 or 30 years! As you surely realize by now, boys and girls both suffer from this captivity to satan, and the enemy builds much different strongholds in girls than he does in boys. We'll discuss these in the next two chapters.

Things to Think About

1. How did Rahab hear about God? What made her trust Him?

2. What change must have occurred in Rahab to change her from a prostitute to the mother of a man like Boaz?

3. How did God look at Rahab even when she was a prostitute? How did He show this?

4. Read Joshua chapters 2 and 6. What was the sign Rahab hung outside her window so that she and her relatives would not be killed when the city fell?

22

Strongholds in Girls

S in always causes death and pain. Hence, a girl who believes the big lie and gives herself sexually to a boy always suffers pain and the destruction of the vision God gave her. When she finds that this boy does not love her as much as the man in her vision, her vision is shattered. Like broken glass, it is hard to put back together again.

This is particularly true because the progress of the lie convinces a girl that her dream was wrong and she is stupid to look for a man who will really love her enough to die for her. This disillusionment begins when she finds out that the boy loves himself more than he loves her. Because this does not match her dream, she knows that she can't really trust him.

As a girl searches for truth, she may become even more enmeshed in the lie and begin to distrust what she thought was truth. Then she starts to think that she has discovered a new "reality." What she has really discovered is the reality of sin and its terrible results. Her discovery and her false understanding take her even farther from God and safety, and death and destruction establish a stronger hold on her. As sin continues to lie to her, building bigger lies that take her farther and farther from God, she loses all protection and moves swiftly toward destruction.

At this point, many thoughts fill a girl's mind: *I have been deceived. Boys cannot be trusted to love and protect me. God cannot be trusted to love and protect me!* Yes, it is true that she has been deceived. Yes, it is true that boys cannot be trusted! (Remember, boys are not men! They have to go through fire to become men.) *No, it is **not** true that God cannot be trusted!*

Never Good Enough
To "Satisfy" Wife

ANXIETY
INSECURITY
MATERIAL LUSTS
HARLOTRY

SPIRIT THAT DEVOURS AND IS *NEVER SATISFIED*

Chief Strongholds in Women from Sexual Immorality

This last lie is the lie that satan most wants to build in all of us. It is the lie he told Eve. *He wants us to take charge of our own lives, thereby refusing to trust and obey God.* He also wants us to make war on the people we love.

Therefore, the evil one continues to speak to the girl's soul, arguing *that **God** cannot be trusted to love and protect her, that **no one** can be trusted to love and care for her, that she must take care of herself.* He wants her to believe that she must be in control. When this happens, she is no longer a free woman, but a slave to the *lie* that she can and must protect herself. Even greater destruction awaits the girl or woman who believes this lie, because it leads her to hate God and men, and to go even farther off on her own. Thinking that her safety is in herself, she neither expects nor accepts love and protection from anyone whom she can't control.

Yet, the first vision the girl received at a young age remains deep in her heart. She is still looking for a man she can trust who will really love her by rescuing her and setting her free. *That man is alive. He is coming for her!*

Until that man comes and tears down the walls that hold her prisoner, satan continues to build his stronghold within her, causing her to make war against a boy and, thus, make herself miserable. The following tactics add to the battle between them:

- The girl tries to control the boy even more because she knows he is not trustworthy.

- The boy responds by withdrawing because he doesn't want to be controlled.

- The boy tries to satisfy his desire for more sex by buying it from the girl with favors and by trying to prove that he loves her.

- The girl knows in her heart that the boy doesn't love her with the love she needs, so nothing he does is good enough.

- Both are discontented: the girl because she knows that she can't control him and, thus, must buy his love, a love that is never good enough; the boy because his desire for sex is never satisfied and he continues the pattern of buying sex through favors and pulling away to resist the girl's control.

The bottom line for girls is *insecurity*. When a girl becomes entrapped in a stronghold of *insecurity*, satan works to convince her that no one other than herself can provide her security. The more she tries to provide for herself, the more the real security she needs evades her. This satisfies satan well. As long as the girl tries to control her security, she cannot receive the security a boy who truly loves her might offer. Thus, she remains satan's captive as she continually becomes more and more deceived, and more and more destroyed.

Still, the girl waits for the man who will prove he really loves her. Her vision of a knight in shining armor is dusty and clouded, but not totally gone. That knight will suffer much to free her.

Things to Think About

1. Do you know girls who behave like the girls described above?

2. What signs of insecurity, if any, do you see in yourself? Do you like them?

3. What kind of girl do you think boys really desire for their wives? Anxious or confident? Fretful or peaceful? Controlling or trusting? Other characteristics?

23

Strongholds in Boys

A boy who believes the lie also suffers pain and destruction. After he has cheated a girl, he knows that he is guilty, that he has violated his trust and honor. Yet, like all little boys, he continues to pretend. Oh, is he ever deceived!

This deception increases as he tries to convince himself and the girl that sex was (and is) okay because he loves her. In his heart he knows that love requires something more, but he isn't sure what. He has not yet learned that *love protects a girl from sin, it doesn't drag her into it.*

At times the boy is able to think clearly about these questions, but his sexual desire often makes him captive to the lies he already believes. He is helpless to stop grabbing selfishly for what he wants. Only more sex seems to satisfy him—for a little while.

So for a while, the boy and the girl may both try to prove that he truly loves her. It's part of the harlotry. They need to cover guilt and trade more sex. Yet he really loves himself, and he knows it. The boy is trapped! How can he admit the lie?

Eventually the boy will tire of proving his love. Then he either leaves the girl or marries her to prove his love once and for all. Right? Wrong! That's what he thinks!

No! If he leaves the girl, he will fall into the same sin cycle over and over again with other girls as he becomes hardened to the lies and destruction of harlotry. Without realizing what is happening to him, he will destroy more girls until girls lose all value to him except for sex! Then he will come to hate what God gave him for blessing.

Never Good Enough
To "Satisfy" Husband

LUST
IMAGININGS
PORNOGRAPHY
SEXUAL PERVERSIONS
HARLOTRY

SPIRIT THAT DEVOURS AND IS *NEVER SATISFIED*

Chief Strongholds in Men from Sexual Immorality

90

If he marries, both the boy and the girl will discover that he has an appetite for sex that cannot be satisfied. What his wife gives to him will never be good enough. Even if she tries with all her heart to satisfy her husband, she will find out that she can't. He will always want more and more.

Before long, the man will use the same methods he first used to get sex. Seduction! Pressure! Accusations that his wife doesn't love him! Lies! Special gifts! Money! All will rain upon the head of the frustrated wife. Even when she allows herself to be pressured into responding, this will not satisfy him!

Harlotry does not satisfy, but a man who is deceived does not see that *he* is the cause of his dissatisfaction. He will blame his wife for his unhappiness. He will begin to think that she is inadequate. He will begin to dream of other women who could satisfy his desires.

As the husband fights his dissatisfaction with the marriage, pinning the blame on his wife, sexual satisfaction becomes his false picture of true contentment and satisfaction. Then the following patterns emerge:

- The husband tries to force his wife to respond to him because she can't give her love freely.

- He becomes angry and refuses to help her because she wants him to prove his love.

- He feels inadequate as a man because she is insecure. (This is *true*.)

- He loses the headship of his household because he is inadequate.

The bottom line for boys is *nurture*. A boy's stronghold is, thus, a perverted *nurture* appetite or a *concupiscence* for sex. He needs nurture, but he doesn't know what it is or where to get it. He is trapped in his fantasies about girls and sex. Though he looks for nurture, he will look in the wrong places and in the wrong ways. More and more turmoil, anger, frustration, and destruction are all he will find.

The husband's problem is compounded by his wife's insecurity. He is married to a girl who has exactly the same problem about her *security*. She has a perverted *security* appetite or a *concupiscence* for security. Thus, their private pain feeds and enlarges the pain of the other in an endless circle of frustration and rage.

The boy in a man's body is impotent, unable to raise up godly seed. Just like the Bible says, he has lost his *strength* and *vigor* (Prov. 5:9-10). No amount of material wealth from the man's hard-earned goods will satisfy his insecure wife. No amount of sex will please the woman's nurture-starved husband. Unless something happens to reverse this spiral of death, both the hard-earned goods and the pleasure of sex will one day be lost.

Like the girl who still holds deep within her a vision of a knight who will rescue and protect her, the boy still wants to do something *great*, although he doesn't have a clue what that means. Only as true nurture touches him and opens his soul will he achieve that long-buried dream.

Things to Think About

1. Have you known a married couple that is locked in the patterns described in this chapter and the previous one?

2. Do you know any marriages that have been restored after they had been destroyed? If so, how?

3. How can children escape the same cycles of sex and insecurity that have destroyed their parents' marriages?

24

Warfare Between Strongholds

Let's take a last look at this failing marriage. We'll consider the bride first.

Is she satisfied and contented? *No, of course not! No woman suffers more than the woman whose husband shows her that she is not good enough!* If she was insecure before marriage, she is even more insecure now. As her insecurity mounts, she loses the ability to express love for her husband.

Remember that a woman is designed like a breast. If a breast is not protected, it is destroyed. Therefore, the more insecure a woman becomes, the more she loses her capacity to give nurture, warmth, and life. She simply dries up as a woman!

Now let's look at the bridegroom. Is his wife confident in his leadership? Does she respect him and submit to his decisions? Does he feel "good enough"? No, not if she doesn't trust him and feel secure in his love. Because she is always anxious, trying to control him, she barters her love for what she wants instead of giving it to him freely.

No man is hurt more than a man whose wife has no confidence in him, who wants only his paycheck! He cannot draw strength and nurture from such a wife, nor will he look forward to coming home to her at the end of each work day. His work is ineffective, his protection absent. How can he even try to provide for a girl who never accepts his efforts as *good enough*? How will he remain faithful to her?

As you can see, the strongholds in the man and the woman work against each other. How can a wife respect and trust a man who fails to protect her and provide for her? How can a husband be encouraged by a wife who neither respects nor trusts him? The man just keeps tearing down his wife, and the woman keeps destroying her husband.

Are they ever at peace? Not for long! Neither of them can find contentment because each is too busy trying to satisfy his or her own needs. As the man struggles to cope with his wife's lack of trust and her anxiety and insecurity, he acts more and more like a little boy. He pouts, he gets angry, he pours out his frustration. Indeed, he acts like King Ahab of Israel when he couldn't get his way (1 Kings 21).

Meanwhile, the woman becomes more and more like Jezebel, King Ahab's wife. She seizes authority in the home and puts down her husband. Indeed, she puts down all men, even men of God, and uses her body to control them, becoming a powerful spiritual force to destroy men. Because she hates men, including her husband, she will turn away from them to draw pleasure and satisfaction from other things. Yet, she will still attempt to use sex like a harlot for the control and the destruction of men (1 Kings 16:31-33; 18:13; 19:1-4; 2 Kings 9:30-37).

Each imprisoned by the lies and strongholds that bind them, the man and his wife will go deeper and deeper into their individual fantasies until they create secret places they would be ashamed to admit to the other. Here is where satan hides and builds his lies.

Satan's lies will lead the man to find other ways of satisfying his appetite for sex. Unsatisfied by his wife's body, sooner or later he will *need* pornography, sexual perversion, sodomy, and adultery.

The chances are good that he will also turn to the molestation of his daughters (if he has any). Eventually his appetite for sex will ruin all the women in his family.

Satan's lies are also active in the woman's thoughts and emotions. What do you suppose she will do with the first man who offers her affection and security? She will commit harlotry with him at the drop of a hat! This can happen after 20 years of marriage! This is her fantasy because harlotry has ruined the wedding bed! The appetite for security that she satisfied with sin now is never satisfied.

So *nurture* wars with *security* as each marriage partner is never satisfied, never contented. As the death march continues, the very thing they originally stole becomes the first to die: their sex life. Can this marriage survive? What will happen to the children who share their parents' pain?

The Bible clearly states that sin multiplies. Sex sin is the worse sin of all. Therefore, the apostle Paul warns us to flee from sexual immorality because "he who sins sexually sins against his own body" (1 Cor. 6:18 NIV).

The lie could never stand if it was brought to light. That's why satan tries to create strongholds within men and women that separate them. That's why he traps us in sinful secrets and shame. Lies do well in darkness and aloneness.

Things to Think About

1. What are the chances that your marriage will survive if you have sex before marriage?

2. What steps are you willing to take to avoid this destruction in your life?

25

Making a Man

I t is so easy to mess up God's design for our lives! We need strong protection to keep nature from taking over and destroying what God means for our good. Both girls and boys need to stay under protection, but boys need one thing more. They need to go through fire. Protection for them is a two-edged sword.

Boys will take anything they can get for free. Men are willing to pay any price to attain what they desire. It takes going through fire to turn a boy into a man!

Boys work hard to avoid going through fire! Who wouldn't? Often this natural tendency is encouraged by women and girls. Because fire goes against their nurturing instinct and increases their insecurity, women and girls are often afraid what fire will do to their husbands, sons, and boyfriends. Thus, mothers work to help their sons avoid testings, and girlfriends try to spare their boyfriends the pain of tribulation. Therefore, women can't apply the fire. It must come from another man.

The Bible tells the story of Jacob and his rotten sons. Jacob was a mama's boy whose mother helped him to steal his brother's blessing. Instead of trusting God to make Jacob into a man in His own time and His own way, Rebekah cheated to get Isaac, her husband, to give Jacob what she believed he needed. Their deception produced disaster! Jacob became an exile from home to escape his brother's wrath. He never saw his mother again.

Even as Jacob had deceived his father, so his mother's brother deceived him. After Jacob had worked for Laban for seven years to earn his beloved Rachel, Laban tricked Jacob and wed him to Rachel's older sister, Leah, instead! Jacob then had to work another seven years for Rachel. Thus, he paid a high price for the woman he loved. This started him on the long road of growth toward manhood.

Unfortunately, Jacob was not able to raise up godly children *because he had refused to trust God to work through Isaac, his father.* In fact, Jacob raised a bunch of kids who committed about every kind of evil you can imagine. The oldest boy slept with one of his dad's concubines (Gen. 35:22), and the next two boys plotted the murder of the men of a whole town because one of the men had raped Dinah, their sister (Gen. 34).

Jacob encouraged further mischief among his children when he favored his eleventh son, Joseph, born to Rachel, the wife he loved, after many years of barrenness. Thus, Jacob played favorites just like his dad had. This made the older brothers hate Joseph.

To save the family, God had to raise up someone who would trust and obey Him. God chose to use Joseph because Jacob had already messed up his daughter and his ten oldest sons. So God took Joseph away from his dad at a young age. Through the fire of slavery and imprisonment, God made Joseph into a real man, a man able to save and preserve life (Gen. 50:20).

When God chose to save Jacob's family through Joseph, He did not abandon Joseph's older brothers. God also took them through fire. This process of going through fire is extremely important in the transformation of a boy into a man. All boys want to be men, but most people, girls and boys alike, do not understand that God builds boys into men by requiring them to be tested and to endure various trials. Instead of avoiding the difficult things God sends their way, boys must embrace them as a necessary part of the maturing process. Women and girls must, likewise, get out of the way and let God prove their husbands, sons, and sweethearts.

The mark of a man is that he will die to rescue and protect the girl (or people) he loves. Boys think this is romantic nonsense, and they assume that girls are expecting too much to believe such a dumb thing. They are wrong! This is not "Mother Goose"; it is the real thing. God's plan to prepare a boy to be truly happy and fulfilled as a man requires a rite of passage through fire. *He must discover that he loves a girl enough to pay any price for her!*

Boys, the process you have to go through will probably not be as bad as what Jacob's sons endured, but it will be rough. That's okay. You were designed by God to become a man. He will help you to achieve His purpose. So get ready!

Can you guess who God will use to apply the fire to you, to refine you, to purify your motives, and to help you discover the truth about yourself and your girl? It will probably be your girl's father. As he is responsible for his daughter's safety, he will require proof from you that you truly love her. Only men can refine other men. Let me explain by telling you the stories of Joseph and Judah.

Things to Think About

1. If you are a girl, do you trust your dad to control your boyfriends? Do you trust God to work through your dad? How about your pastor or your brothers? Is there any man you trust to do this for you?

26

Making Men: Joseph

Method One

The stories of Joseph and Judah show two tough methods by which God produces real men who can do what is right by people and by God. Joseph and Judah were brothers, two of twelve sons born to their father, Jacob. As we saw in the last chapter, Jacob was a weak father. He had been raised as a mama's boy who lied to his father, cheated his brother, and ran away to escape his problems. Because he was corrupted, he was easy to cheat. He spent most of his adult years unable to protect himself or his family. His daughter was raped and his corrupted sons committed nearly every sin in the book. This continued until God intervened through the person of Joseph.

The ten older brothers were jealous of Joseph because he was their father's favorite. Therefore, they sought to kill him. One day they had their opportunity and nearly did kill him; but at the last minute they changed their minds and sold Joseph into slavery instead. Then they went home and lied to their father that Joseph had been killed by lions (Gen. 37). This happened when Joseph was quite young.

Starting with the mistreatment from his brothers, Joseph learned how to do right without the support of others, even when he was treated unfairly. Joseph did well as a slave in Egypt. He worked hard for Potiphar, his master, who came to recognize that God caused everything that Joseph worked on to prosper. Before long, Potiphar put Joseph in charge of everything in his house. Then Joseph encountered the temptation to sin against his master and against God through sexual sin.

Potiphar's wife asked Joseph to have sex with her, but he refused saying, "My master has withheld nothing from me except you, because you are his wife. How then could I do such a wicked thing and sin against God?" (Gen. 39:9b NIV) When he refused her day after day, she finally framed him and lied to her husband that Joseph had tried to sleep with her. Potiphar, burning with anger against Joseph, threw him into the king's prison. There, too, God showed Joseph favor so that he was soon put in charge of all the prisoners (Gen. 39:19-23).

While he was in jail, Joseph correctly interpreted the dreams of two other prisoners. He predicted that one servant of the king would be killed and the other would be forgiven and restored to his job. All happened as Joseph had said.

Two years later, the man who had been restored to his position happened to be with Pharaoh, the king of Egypt, when Pharaoh had a dream that his magicians could not interpret. Then the king's servant remembered Joseph and how he had correctly interpreted his dream. When he told Pharaoh about Joseph, Pharaoh ordered that Joseph should be brought to him.

After he had listened to Pharaoh's dream, Joseph said the dream meant that there would be seven years of plentiful harvest followed by seven years of famine. Then he advised Pharaoh to appoint commissioners over the land who would set aside food during the years of plenty to feed the people during the years of famine. Pharaoh believed Joseph's interpretation of his dream and put him in charge of the whole project. Thus, Joseph was put in charge of all Egypt, right under the Pharaoh himself (see Gen. 40-41).

Joseph reached manhood by learning to do right even when there was no one to appreciate his trustworthiness and by refusing to engage in sexual immorality. These are the marks of a real man. How easy it would have been for Joseph to feel sorry for himself, to hate his brothers because they had sold him into slavery, or to take what Potiphar's wife so blatantly offered him. This would have been the response of the average man. Joseph proved himself to be a real man by refusing to give in to any of these temptations, even though he was alone; *there were no friends to help him do what was right.*

Girls want a man who will do right, who will deny himself for her sake. Yet, like Potiphar's wife, they often use their bodies to entice boys who are growing into manhood. It takes a strong man who loves something more than himself and his own pleasure to withstand this temptation. No woman should try to destroy such a man. Sexual temptation is a dreadful fire to endure.

Some men obtain manhood this way. They pass through the fire by denying lies, deceit, and ungodly sexual gratification. Other boys grow into manhood by being restored after they have been corrupted, as in the case of Judah. Let's study the story of Judah. Then you decide which fiery passage you recommend.

Things to Think About

1. Why would a girl try to entice an upright man to have sex with her? Do you think more than physical pleasure might be involved? Might she be trying to gain ownership or control over the man?

2. What might have been going through Joseph's brothers' minds while Joseph was a slave and a prisoner in Egypt?

3. How did the famine affect Joseph's brothers? Who was truly in control of the events in Joseph's life and the lives of his brothers?

27

Making Men: Judah

Method Two

Judah was the fourth son of Jacob. The first ten sons had no regard for their father and did pretty much as they pleased. The oldest son slept with his father's concubine (his brothers' mom), and the next two murdered the men of an entire city because one of its men had raped their sister, after which all the sons looted the city. Judah bought sex with a harlot, and all ten brothers sold Joseph into slavery and lied to their dad.

Does this sound like a family you'd like to live in? I doubt it. These brothers were "buzzard meat," like dead, decayed food for vultures. But God had a plan for them. Through this plan, Judah would become a true man.

When the famine hit and Jacob's family ran out of food, they heard that there was plenty of food for sale in Egypt. So off they went to Egypt, leaving Benjamin, their father's favorite son now that Joseph had "died," at home with their father. When the brothers arrived in Egypt and bowed before the Egyptian official who sold the grain, they did not recognize their brother Joseph. Joseph, however, recognized them and determined to see if they had changed since he had last seen them. Thus, he kept his identity secret and devised a plan to put pressure on them. First, he made them afraid of him by accusing them of being spies and by throwing them all in jail! (Keep in mind that Joseph was a man submitted to God's authority. Therefore, he could accurately hear God as He directed Joseph's actions toward his brothers.)

While his brothers were in Egypt, Joseph found out enough from them to know that they had lied to their dad about what had happened to him. He also discovered that his younger brother, Benjamin, was still alive. So, Joseph put pressure on his brothers by holding Simeon as a prisoner until the others brought Benjamin down to Egypt. Warning them not to return to Egypt without Benjamin, Joseph bound Simeon, filled each man's sack with grain, gave them provisions for the journey, and sent them on their way. (Of course, Joseph knew that the famine would last for seven years and they would certainly run out of food again!) Joseph also did another thing. He secretly gave orders that each man's money should be placed in his sack.

So Joseph's brothers went home with fear in their hearts, remembering what they had done to Joseph years before. When they stopped for the night and one brother discovered his money in the mouth of his sack, the combination of pressure and undeserved blessing did something unusual to them. For the first time in their lives, Joseph's brothers began to fear God (Gen. 42:28).

If you read Genesis chapters 41 through 45, you will soon see that father Jacob still indulged in pity parties. Feeling sorry for himself, he blamed his sons for his many sorrows: "You have bereaved me of my children: Joseph is no more, and Simeon is no more, and you would take Benjamin; all these things are against me" (Gen. 42:36b). Thus, he refused to let Benjamin return to Egypt with his brothers.

Eventually Jacob's family again ran out of food. No one could persuade him to let Benjamin accompany his brothers to Egypt to get more food. Indeed, Jacob complained that they had even mentioned Benjamin to the Egyptian official (Gen. 43:6).

Earlier, the oldest son, Reuben, had made a stupid offer to let Jacob kill his two sons if he didn't bring Benjamin home safely. Finally, Judah made an offer to his father that unlocked Jacob's heart and helped him to let go of his most precious possession. Here are Judah's words: "Send the lad with me and we will arise and go, that we may live and not die, we as well as you and our little ones. I myself will be surety [ransom] for him; you may hold me responsible for him. If I do not bring him back to you and set him before you, then let me bear the blame before you forever" (Gen. 43:8b-9).

Can you hear the great power in Judah's words? Who knows if Judah expected that he would have to give up his life to keep his promise, but the fact is that he set *himself* as the guarantee of Benjamin's safety.

Suddenly Jacob came back to life and agreed that his sons should return to Egypt with Benjamin. He also told them to take double the money that had been returned in their sacks, as well as many nice gifts for Pharaoh. As Jacob waved good-bye to Benjamin and the others, he thought that he might well lose Benjamin forever.

During this second trip to Egypt, Joseph was very nice to his brothers and gave them a big feast. But this time before they started home, Joseph not only gave orders that each man's money should be placed in the mouth of his sack, he also told his servants to put his own silver cup in Benjamin's sack to frame him for stealing!

Shortly after the brothers had left town, Joseph's servant caught up with them and accused them of taking his master's cup. The hearts of the brothers must have sank as the servant searched their sacks, for they thought they had escaped. When the cup turned up in Benjamin's sack, they were overcome with their past guilt over Joseph. They knew they were guilty and that God had overtaken their evil with His penalty. Therefore, they were willing to be slaves—along with Benjamin—for the rest of their lives. Returning to Egypt, Judah spoke for the brothers, offering all as slaves, not just the youngest in whose sack the cup had been found.

Joseph replied, "No! That's not fair! I can't do such a thing! Go on home to your dad. I'll just keep Benjamin as my slave!"

Wow! Talk about pressure! Now they could confess what they had done when they sold Joseph into slavery! They could go home and tell their father that Benjamin was a *slave*! Only this time it would be the truth, and it even looked like Benjamin was guilty. What a temptation to give up and go home to the wife and family!

This is how it is with sin. Each time it gets harder and harder to get things right! Joseph knew this. Therefore, he had set up another opportunity for his brothers to repeat their crime against him.

It's hard to say what went through each brother's mind as he listened to Joseph's words. But we know that one man at least had developed a heart of real love for his father. Also, he had truly repented of his sin against Joseph and his father. Now he was ready to die for his father and his youngest brother. Thus, Judah asked to talk alone with the Egyptian official.

The moving words of Judah recorded in Genesis 44:18-34 express Judah's love for his father, reveal his guarantee of safety for Benjamin, and display his anguish should he need to return to his father without Benjamin. He offered himself as a slave in Benjamin's place! Joseph was so moved by his brother's plea that he burst into tears and bawled loudly before his brothers. When he told them who he was, they were speechless, unable to believe it!

This whole story is so incredible! Through Joseph, Jacob and all the families of Joseph's brothers moved to Egypt (where they stayed for 400 years). Years later, when Jacob was about to die, he spoke prophecies over each of his boys, reserving the best of God's promises for Joseph and Judah. Joseph's line inherited the promise of material wealth and riches. Judah's line received the spiritual promise that the Messiah, the Son of God who would give up His life for our eternal ransom, would come from his family.

Girls, do you see what happened to Judah? Boys, do you? He learned to put the happiness of others before his own, even if it cost him his life. This is the chief issue of manhood. It is the only way a boy or a corrupted man can become a true man.

All men and boys face this decision, although this choice may never be explained to you this way again. Can you look beyond yourself to the welfare of others? Are you willing to give up your life as a ransom for someone else's happiness? This is the rite of passage to becoming a man.

Those men who choose to give themselves for their wives and children will find that they possess the wisdom, strength, and power to be a shield for their families. Like Joseph (and Boaz) or Judah, they will be seasoned through fire into mature men. Both methods work wonderfully. Both methods are *hard*! Indeed, they are much the same. There is no other way.

Things to Think About

1. Think again about the story *Beauty and the Beast*. What was the Beast like before he became a beast? When did he become perfected into a real man?

2. Boys, if you were given the choice, would you choose to be perfected into manhood like Joseph or Judah? Girls, which method would you prefer?

3. Can a boy become a man without enduring pressure and fire?

28

More About God's Design

This book started by talking about how God describes Himself in the Bible and how He designed us to share His likeness. Even though sin has scarred us badly and it causes us to want to run away from God, He is faithful to keep on loving us until we are convinced that He loves us. When we become convinced, we become "believers."

One of the beauties of God's creation is the story of the gospel—the good news of the chief Bridegroom, Jesus Christ, who rescues us from death. The story of the gospel is told nearly everywhere: in nature,[1] in the scientific laws of the universe,[2] in the stars,[3] in our own lives, and in the Bible.

God imprinted on girls' hearts the entire story of the gospel. He intends for them to discover its beauty and power by living as

---

1.　See *Character Sketches*, Volumes I, II, and III, (Oakbrook, Illinois: Institute in Basic Life Conflicts).
2.　See Henry Morris, *The Bible and Science*, (Grand Rapids: Baker Book House); Dr. Hugh Ross, *The Fingerprint of God*, (Orange, California: Promise Publishing Co.).
3.　See Kenneth Fleming, *God's Voice in the Stars*, (Neptune, New Jersey: Loizeaux Brothers, Inc.).

111

real brides of heroic bridegrooms. In a similar manner, God has given boys the ability to discover what being *heroic* really means. His plan for each boy includes the joy of winning a bride's love by giving her his own proof of love.

It's no fun to die. In some ways, boys have the more difficult task. A boy does not have a girl's vision to see what the future holds for him, but after he has paid the price for winning his sweetheart's love and her hand in marriage, he will "see [the results] and be satisfied" (Is. 53:11). There's joy on the other side.

Both boys and girls can see God's truth in their lives and marriages, including everything God has told us about sin and its effect on us. God will be glorified whether we have soft hearts toward Him and respond to Him, or whether we harden our hearts and go our own way, far from Him. The rewards for us, however, are not the same. The joys of obedience to God are easy to see in our world, as are the penalties of disobedience. Just look around you.

The same soul-bonding laws that we talked about earlier in the book concerning men and women also apply to our relationship with God. We declared that a woman is bonded to a man through sex—especially to the first man with whom she has intercourse—and a man is bonded to a woman by risking much for her—by going through fire and paying a ransom for her.

We also used the examples of Boaz and Joseph to show how a man must go first, take the risk, and pay a great price to prove his love. He does this by denying himself, by keeping himself sexually pure, and by accepting transformation by fire. Only after he has been forged through fire into a righteous man can he rescue his bride and set her free.

Jesus is our Bridegroom (Jn. 3:29). He has gone first, risked much, and paid the price to claim us as His bride. He loved us and died for us long before any of us knew Him or cared about Him, even while we hated Him (Rom. 5:8). Jesus is the proof of what men can be.

What kind of love is this? There is no greater love (Jn. 15:13)! Jesus bonded to us when He paid His own life to ransom us from sin and death. He established the New Covenant (a marriage covenant) and sealed it with His blood. He remained true to His commitment and accepted death of His human body and soul. He proved that His love is the real thing.

Jesus will never leave or forsake us. No way could He walk away from us after paying such a high price! Thus, Jesus is bonded to us forever.

The question of supreme importance, then, is not whether Jesus is bonded to us, but, "Are we are bonded to Jesus"? Indeed, how do we become bonded to Him? The answer is the same for all who believe: We bond to God when we receive His Seed—when we agree to have Jesus come into our hearts and live; when we trust Him and open ourselves to Him; when we accept the work of the Holy Spirit in our lives, even as the virgin Mary accepted the Spirit's work in her womb, saying, "May it be done to me according to your word" (Lk. 1:38).

Yes! Our bonding to God is exactly the same! When we receive Him, the power of His nature and life come into us! His living reproductive Seed is placed in the womb of our hearts.

A woman's womb is but a picture of how we receive true life from the Living God through the Bridegroom. Through Jesus, we are bonded to our Maker and our Shield. By taking the Lord Jesus into our hearts, our souls, our innermost beings, we are bonded to our Bridegroom. The marriage is consummated. Our Lord and Savior becomes our Husband forever.

Things to Think About

1. Describe what happens in your heart as you consider the above words. Does Luke 24:32 apply? Does Isaiah 53:1 apply?

29

Patterns of Truth

G od has imprinted many things on our hearts to help us see the truth. Before we conduct an experiment, let me ask you a few questions.

You know what exact opposites are, right? You also know what opposite and equal mean. Okay. Tell me, then, if *light* and *darkness* are exactly opposite and equal.

Most people say right away that *light* and *darkness* are, indeed, opposite and equal. They're not. How can I tell this? Well, suppose you bring a light into the presence of darkness. What happens? Does the darkness win or the light?

It's obvious, isn't it? Light always conquers darkness. The only way darkness can stay even with light is if the two are kept separate and light is not brought into the darkness.

What else might this first illustration reflect? What does your spirit say about light and darkness?

Now let's look at the concepts of *truth* and *lies*. Are these exactly opposite and equal? Most teens would say yes right away, but if we look more closely, we soon discover that truth and lies are not opposite and equal.

Can truth exist without a lie? Well, sure! Is the reverse true? No! Before there can be a lie, a truth must first be established. The whole concept of a *lie* depends on the prior existence of a *truth*. A lie is simply a truth that has been distorted. Once a truth has been established, many lies can be told against it. This does not change the truth; it still remains but one truth. *Truth always exists first and stands by itself, regardless of how many lies, if any, may be told against it.*

Now let's consider a third pair. Let's compare *things that are seen* with *things that are unseen*. Are these equal and opposite? Some teens I've spoken to have good insight. (Perhaps they've been sharpened up a bit by the first two questions!) They know right away that the *seen* is not equal to and opposite from the *unseen*. One support for this argument is the Bible verse: "For the things which are seen are temporal [temporary], but the things which are not seen are eternal [exist forever]" (2 Cor. 4:18b).

Okay, what else? What more can we say about the relationship between the seen world and the unseen world? Are they opposites or do they reflect the same truth and light, lies and darkness? Does the temporary world reflect the eternal world, or vice versa? These are questions for which God will eventually give you the answers, if you seek them.

Now let's consider an experiment involving a group of people. Say you have three or four dozen people sitting on the floor of a large room. Now pick a boy and a girl (age makes no difference as long as they are the same age) and give them this problem:

> You have to hike through 50 miles of desert. All these people sitting on the floor represent rocks and bushes in the desert. Your task is to go through this desert in which there are rattlesnakes hiding under the rocks and behind the bushes. You have 15 seconds to work out how the two of you will do this. (Pause). Now walk out through these people single file. Ready? Go!

Run this experiment two or three times. If possible, change the ages of the participants each time, keeping them matched in age. Ask the people on the floor to watch what happens; see if they can pick out the pattern that usually occurs. Can you guess what this pattern is?

"...behold, a white horse, and He who sat upon it is called faithful and True...." (Revelation 19:11)

The boy will usually hesitate, and the girl will say to him, "You go first." Finally, the boy will go first, followed by the girl. What can we see from this?

For the most part, men know what is right, but they need encouragement to do it. Women are also quick to see what is right. They know that men should go first and protect them, and they are quick to encourage them to do this. Thus, both men and women know that it is right for a man to go first into danger.

Some people say this is a learned response. I don't think so. I believe it is a reflection of truth, light given for our benefit to reflect the design of the unseen world into our temporary world. It portrays a powerful principle of the Designer's own nature and His plan for how the bridegroom (the man) should live with the bride (the woman). The bridegroom takes the bite of the serpent so the bride goes free! This is the eternal truth of the unseen world (Gen. 3:15)!

If the man goes first through rattlesnake-infested land, who is most likely to run into a rattlesnake and get bitten? The man, of course! Why do men and women both agree that this pattern of the man going first is right? Because God has written this on our hearts. Though it may be difficult for the man to do, it is right that he should go first. God ordained it this way.

Here's another interesting discovery. When a group of teenagers is asked to describe and confirm the vision given to all girls (see Chapter 1), nearly all the girls will agree in their description, even those who have already been damaged by boys and thereby have lost some or most of their vision. Few boys, however, will agree with the girls' description of their vision. Most boys think that a girl's vision of a knight who will rescue and protect her is romantic nonsense, a fairy tale that cannot come true. They also would disagree with a girl's idea that it is possible for a man to find fulfillment by taking the bite of the snake to protect and save his girl.

Why can girls see this but boys cannot? This happens because God has given girls the opportunity to know the gospel of God in Jesus Christ in their hearts while they are still girls, but boys must become men before they can understand and accept it. A boy knows in his heart that he is destined by God to do something

"And He laid hold of the dragon, the serpent of old, who is the devil and satan, and bound him for a thousand years." (Revelation 20:2)

TRUE LOVE   **COURAGE**
FAITHFULNESS   **VISION**

Jesus

great with his life, but he doesn't know what that great thing will be. If he knew that greatness comes to men as they die to win and protect their brides, he would not be able to bear it.

A boy cannot carry the weight of being the bridegroom until he becomes a man and is brought to the point where he cherishes his bride more than his own life.[1] This is why a boy must remain accountable to a man, usually his girl's father, until he is ready to give and dedicate himself completely to his girl. As he remains under the authority of the man who is superior in loving and protecting the girl, the boy becomes perfected in his own flesh until he is ready to be the girl's bridegroom, and she is granted to him in marriage.

Things to Think About

1. In the gospel of Jesus Christ, who is the Bridegroom? Where does the Bible teach this?

2. To increase your understanding of the relationship between a girl's vision and God's plan of salvation for mankind, connect the concept on the left to the correct Bible verse on the right. Some may be used more than once.

a)	The White Horse	1)	Revelation 19:7-9
b)	The Dragon	2)	Galatians 4:22-31
c)	The Bridegroom (bright as "the sun")	3)	Revelation 20
d)	The Rider of the Horse: "Faithful and True"	4)	Psalm 19:1-6
e)	The Bride (who makes herself ready)	5)	Ephesians 5:25-33
f)	The Free Woman (by promise, not "works")	6)	Revelation 19:11-14

---

1. Read Ephesians 5:25-33 to help you understand this concept better. Even Jesus was perfected in the flesh as a man by offering His life on the cross as a sacrifice to save and win His eternal Bride, the Church (Heb. 5:8-9). All bridegrooms must make this sacrifice.

3. Why is the Bridegroom referred to as "the Lamb"? Does this have anything to do with the price He paid for His Bride?

4. How does the Bride of Jesus Christ know her true value? Is this based on the Bride's value system or the Bridegroom's? How, then, should I value myself? How should you value yourself?

5. What is your value according to the Word of God?

A Summary of Lies That Destroy Teens

Thus far, we have discussed many things in this book. Now I want to summarize some of the most significant lies that destroy the happiness of young people. We will enumerate lies that primarily affect girls or boys, then we will list some lies that affect both genders equally.

Lies That Tempt Girls to Mess Up Their Future Happiness

- I have to prove my love for my boyfriend by having sex with him.

- My boyfriend can't help his sex urge. The only way he can be satisfied is if I give myself to him sexually.

- Since females are designed to satisfy men sexually, it is okay if I do what I want to with my boyfriend.

- If I give myself to my boyfriend sexually, he will be drawn into a deeper relationship with me. Our sexual intimacy will increase his commitment to me, and he will bond to me.

- My boyfriend doesn't need to prove he loves me. I can trust him.

- As long as I don't have a baby, and my boyfriend and I don't mistreat each other, there are no consequences to having sex.

- I don't need the protection of my father. I can take care of myself.

- I can tell whether or not my boyfriend is sincere.

- If I make things too difficult for my boyfriend, I'll lose him. That's bad.

- I can make my boyfriend (or husband) into the person I want him to be.

- As long as I really believe, things will work out no matter what I do.

- If men can't be trusted, then neither can God.

Lies That Tempt Boys to Mess Up Their Future Happiness

- I'm not much of a man if I can't get her to sleep with me. My friends would laugh at me if they knew.

- If she loves and trusts me, she should prove it by sleeping with me.

- Having sex is okay as long as no one gets visibly hurt.

- I can't help myself or stop once I get excited (unless her parents show up!).

- No one needs to hold me accountable. I can figure things out for myself.

- She's just playing hard to get until I convince her that I love her.

- If I tell her I love her and I want to marry her, it'll be okay.

- It's good for me to want to sleep with a girl before I marry her.

- I'll prove I love her after I have sex with her (or marry her).

- I'll do anything as long as I get sex with her. It's worth it.

- She should trust my promises, not my actions.

- God is far away. I won't face any penalties for this.

Lies That Both Boys and Girls Believe

- Both the girl and the boy must prove their love.

- Sex is the answer to the same needs of both boys and girls.

- Sex outside marriage increases a girl's security.

- Sex outside marriage increases a boy's contentment.

- Guilt is only a state of the mind. It is not real, but is shaped by attitude.

- Sexual immorality does not lead to the death of people or relationships.

- A man can be changed if he is held accountable by a good woman.

- Sex proves love.

- Good and evil are concepts defined by man. The nature and definition of sin changes with time, place, and society's standards.

- Acceptance by friends is the most important thing.

- Standards of behavior and ways of protecting them are not important. We can "make things up as we go."

- The future is far away and not worth worrying about. Why shouldn't I have what I want now?

Surely there are other lies that teens and young adults believe in addition to those I have listed. A complete list is not the vital issue here. If you see the falsehood in these statements and agree that the truth of God is different from these, then you are beginning to gird your loins (the vital area around your sex organs) with *truth*, as the apostle Paul admonishes us in the Bible, in Ephesians 6:14.

Now you must put on the breastplate of righteousness and clothe your feet with the gospel of peace so that you may walk in peace, righteousness, and protection. This is our topic for the final chapters of this book.

Things to Think About

1. Do you believe that the Bible tells and describes the truth? Can this truth save us? Read each lie above and state the truth it perverts.

2. What is the connection, if any, between the lies girls often believe and the lie Eve believed when the serpent deceived her? (See Genesis 3:1-6.)

3. What is the connection, if any, between the lies boys believe and their dependency on females for nurture? Are the lies boys believe deep and complicated like the lie Eve believed, or simple like Adam's fall? How are the lies boys believe similar to the fall of Adam?

31

A Summary of Truth and Life for Teens

There is a Man. He called Himself *Truth* and *Life* and *Light*. He also referred to Himself as *the Way*. Not only did He say that He would show us the way, teach us truth, and illustrate life and light for us, He said that He **is** *the Way, the Truth and the Life*. This Man, Jesus, is the *Light of the world*. His life *is the light of men*. (See the Gospel of John in the Bible, chapters 1, 8, 14, and 15.)

Whether you are a girl or a boy, God sent His Son, Jesus, as your Bridegroom. He is the Lamb of God who gave His life as a ransom for you. He is trustworthy. He has proven His love for you. You can depend on Him.

Jesus is alive. He has risen from the dead and sits at the right hand of God making intercession for you, His bride. He has planned the marriage supper. He is eager to reproduce His life in you so that the marriage may be successful and happy.

God the Father and God the Son have determined your value. They have set the price for your ransom as the death of God's Son and the suffering He endured for sin before He died and was resurrected. This is what you are worth. Don't forget it. You are worth the whole price God paid for you because He said it and He paid it!

Jesus did not ransom you with money. His lifeblood was the price of your freedom from death and sin. His death and lifeblood prove your value. His death proves God's love for you. Only His life, freely given because He loves you, could set you free—and it has!

Jesus has given you not only His life but His light and His truth. They alone are your ticket into God's presence. In Jesus, the Son of God, is all truth. In Him you receive the way of protection against all lies. Apart from Him, lies and death will enslave you. You have no protection from them.

You are not saved from death only once. A bride lives with her bridegroom day after day. In a similar manner, you are saved from death repeatedly and forever. In Jesus Christ you are freed from the penalty of all your mistakes—past, present, and future. In Jesus, your destiny has been fixed once and for all. In Jesus, you can be all that you were created to be, all that God intended when He gave you the breath of life.

The Bible clearly reveals God's intention for marriage and the relationship between a man and a woman. It also demonstrates how sexual sin destroys both the marriage relationship and the individual marriage partners. Yet, the significance of this understanding is lost if we apply it only to the relationship between a man and a woman. Yes, the man must be a shield, a sentry, a protector, a covering, a forgiver of sin, and a bearer of iniquity for his bride. Yes, the woman needs the man's protection and forbearance to be a life-giving breast to him. This is all true, but it itself is not Truth.

Only Jesus is Truth. To have Him is to have Truth. To know Him is to know Truth. This knowing is not a casual acquaintance, but a relationship that lasts throughout this life and far beyond. You can have Jesus for all eternity by accepting Him as your Bridegroom and living with Him in intimate, personal fellowship.

When we consider how easily we are deceived and how help-less we are without God's protection, we do well to thank God for His provision for sin. Forgiveness for all our sin is given in Jesus Christ. When we have the Shield, we have everything!

Jesus is *Life*. He is Nurturer, Healer, and Life-Giver. He is the Seed of woman and El-Shadday, the all-sufficient Breast. In Him all life begins and is sustained.

We are patterned after God's first Son. We too can live as brides and bridegrooms according to God's design. God does not lie! His promises to us are sincere and trustworthy. Our design as men and women reflects the *truth* and *life* found in Jesus Christ!

When a man has Christ as his Bridegroom, he is capable of being a successful bridegroom to a woman. When a woman has Christ, she is capable of being a nurturing bride for her groom. Christ makes the difference. He embodies the essential qualities of both men and women.

Do you want a blessed marriage? Take Jesus as your Bride-groom. Believe and obey Him. Accept His protection from the lies and deception of the one who seeks to destroy you. Jesus protects perfectly.

In Christ you will find satisfaction. He will fulfill His many promises for your life. If you have never received Christ as your Savior and Bridegroom, now is the acceptable time, now is the day of salvation, now is the moment of decision. Unite yourself with the Faithful and True, the heavenly Bridegroom who gave Himself for you, by praying the prayer that follows. If you have previously accepted Jesus' proposal of marriage but your relationship with Him is not all it could be, I invite you to renew your relationship with the Savior of the world by pledging yourself to Him anew through the prayer that follows. *Please pray this out loud to bring agreement between your mouth and your heart.*

Dear *Jesus*, Son of God,

You are my eternal Bridegroom. You paid for me with Your life to have me as Your own. Because You didn't leave me in prison to die, but decided I was worth the price, I'm free. I'm free from sin! Thank you, dear Jesus!

Take me to be Your bride; I'm Yours alone. No longer do I belong to satan or the world; I've been rescued by You, my Knight in Shining Armor. Thank you for slaying the dragon, satan, on my behalf. I know You love me.

Now I open my heart to You. I'm Your bride and I want to pour out my life on You. Fill me, place Your *life* in me, reproduce Yourself within me, make me like You. I want other people to see You in me; I want to be pleasing to You. I love You.

Thank you, dear Husband, for searching for me until I could see You and believe in You and Your love. Give me Your Word as my bread of life. Help me to love You in every way possible. Don't ever let me go—You've promised this. Thank you.

Amen.

Did you pray this prayer out loud? If not, what kept you from doing this? Did a thought discourage you? Is such a thought working for or against you? Satan is renounced in the name of Jesus! Please go back and pray this prayer out loud, standing up or kneeling down to help you do it. (If you would like a Scripture to help you do this and understand the importance of doing it, you may find one in Romans 10:8-11.) Then tell your parents, your friends, your pastor—all of them!!!

After praying this prayer out loud, please sign and date the following marriage commitment to Jesus Christ.

Bridegroom's Signature _____ **(Date)** _____

Bride's Signature _____ **(Date)** _____

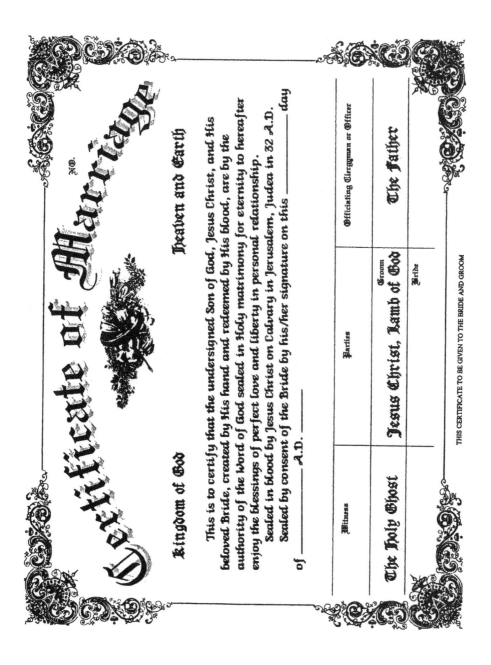

Certificate of Marriage

№.

Kingdom of God

Heaven and Earth

This is to certify that the undersigned Son of God, Jesus Christ, and His beloved Bride, created by His hand and redeemed by His blood, are by the authority of the Word of God sealed in Holy matrimony for eternity to hereafter enjoy the blessings of perfect love and liberty in personal relationship.

Sealed in blood by Jesus Christ on Calvary in Jerusalem, Judea in 32 A.D.

Sealed by consent of the Bride by his/her signature on this _____ day

of _____ A.D. _____

Witness	Parties	Officiating Clergyman or Officer
	Groom	
The Holy Ghost	Jesus Christ, Lamb of God	The Father
	Bride	

THIS CERTIFICATE TO BE GIVEN TO THE BRIDE AND GROOM

131

32

A Final Review of a Girl's Vision

Some details of the vision that God gives to girls are worth reviewing. Examining them again can encourage a girl to stay under the protection God has prepared for her as she journeys on her way toward finding God's bridegroom for her.

First, the girl does not fight the dragon—not at all! This work is done totally by the man God sends for her. Even though she may worry about his health and safety, she cannot fight the dragon herself or help the man fight it. This would be foolishness because it would put her in danger and make it more difficult for her man to win her freedom. She may pray for him and encourage him, but overcoming the dragon is strictly his job.

Second, the girl does not climb down from the castle; the boy must always come up to her. No matter what obstacles may confront him, he must face them and overcome them. Only then can he accomplish what God requires of all boys who would win their girls!

Learn from the example of a butterfly. If you help a butterfly emerge from its cocoon by cutting the cocoon, it will die. It needs the struggle of freeing itself from the cocoon to develop its muscles so it can fly. The same is true for a bridegroom becoming a man.

Although a girl may not realize it, the very castle that seems to imprison her also protects her. As long as she remains there she is safe. If she leaves the castle before her potential protector rescues her, she loses both her protection and the assurance that her protector is equal to the fight. Too often girls who leave the castle before their bridegroom comes for them mess up their futures. Like Eve, they are deceived and destroyed.

Usually the knight in a girl's vision is so far away that he can't talk to his bride while he's fighting for her. Boys will try to talk a girl down from the castle or they will look for a shortcut to avoid the dragon, but knights never do. They are willing to pay the price to *win*, not steal, their princesses.

When a knight finally gets to his girl, he will offer her his arm. When she says yes by taking it, both the knight and his princess know that they belong together for the rest of their lives. Marriage built on this foundation is rich and full. Though life will undoubtedly send difficulties their way, that couple whose marriage is based on the knight's giving of himself for his bride—and the bride's pouring out all her love on her knight—need not fear. Since God has provided the vision, He is able to keep it and fulfill it. All who place their trust in Him will discover that He is faithful to fulfill what He has promised.

This is my desire for all young couples who pledge their love and share the marriage bed. May you know with certainty that you belong to each other forever. Place your trust in God and He will do the rest.

Things to Think About

1. Have you heard of the constellations *Virgo*, *Draco*, and *Orion*? Do you know what these names mean? If not, look them up in a dictionary. How do they relate to the Bible or to this story?

2. If scientists proved that the universe began at a specific time, and that it was created out of nothing, would this change your thinking about God?

3. If God proved to you personally that He loves you, and that He will care for you and provide for all your needs, would this change the way you think about Him?

4. Do you think God can show Himself wonderful by using the hard-hearted as well as the soft-hearted?

33

A Final Review of a Boy's Desire

Many men never satisfy their desire to do something great. They go through their entire lives without finding what God placed in their hearts. Although they know when they are boys that they are destined for greatness, and they want to fulfill that destiny, they never discover what that greatness is or how they can attain it.

This is what causes the so-called *midlife crisis* of many men. They feel frustrated because they've never found greatness. In fact, many men believe that they have wasted their lives because of this.

It is true that few men have specific desires to become the President of the United States or to be an astronaut or an Olympic champion (though some may attain this), yet they all sense that they have missed the essence and purpose of life. By the time these men reach the age of 50, they doubt whether they have done anything of value and worth. This is what bothers them.

If you asked each man and boy to tell you who determines greatness, few would respond: "God is the One who determines what is great." Therein lies the problem. Most men do not understand that God is the One who determines greatness and places satisfaction in the heart.

The spirit is willing, but the flesh is weak. Men resist the truth when it comes to the greatness God intends for them, because they think it is too hard. They avoid going through the door of greatness because they are afraid of dying. They fear what they might have to give up to fight for a girl and win. Instead, they expect to love and be loved without making a sacrifice.

Too often girls help boys avoid the dragon. They encourage them to detour the issues and avoid the battle. Such selfishness kills. It takes away the opportunity for greatness.

God sets the standards for greatness and gives each man the opportunity to "get it right." He gives him one chance to be a Joseph. If a man messes up and ruins his sexual purity, he can no longer be a Joseph. Yet, he may become a Judah by offering himself as a ransom for someone else.

How does God measure greatness? Who is the standard against which all men are measured? Jesus, the Bridegroom, is God's measure of greatness. The Bible clearly details this standard against which all men are measured.

Have this attitude in yourselves which was also in Christ Jesus, who, although He existed in the form of God, did not regard equality with God a thing to be grasped, but emptied Himself, taking the form of a bond-servant, and being made in the likeness of men. Being found in appearance as a man, He humbled Himself by becoming obedient to the point of death, even death on a cross.

For this reason also, God highly exalted Him, and bestowed on Him the name which is above every name, that at the name of Jesus every knee will bow, of those who are in heaven and on earth, and under the earth, and that every tongue will confess that Jesus Christ is Lord, to the glory of God the Father (Philippians 2:5-11).

Many men who have put off until the age of 50 the decision to give themselves up for their wives think they must leave their wives to find their greatness. Nothing could be farther from the truth. Actually, God is calling them to turn to their wives and do what they should have done long ago—to deny themselves and give all that they have and are to protect and defend the bride of their youth.

Things to Think About

1. If you are a girl, list some reasons why you should not help your boyfriend avoid giving himself up for you. How can you keep yourself from interfering with God's plan?

2. If you are a boy, describe what happens when you avoid doing a job your father told you to do. What happens the longer you put it off? Do you think Judah's process was harder or easier than Joseph's?

3. How can God help each of us fulfill His purposes for our lives? What might be the key to this victory?

34

Restoration

The primary purpose of this book is to help teens who have not yet destroyed their sexual purity find *true* reasons and *true* power to resist the lies that buffet them and draw them toward destruction through sexual immorality. Sex is God's gift for the full satisfaction of love and reproduction within a marriage covenant only. Sex under any other conditions leaves both the boy and the girl unprotected and open to great devastation.

If you understand the lies that draw you into sexual immorality and the destruction that the abuse of sex brings to your future, find ways with your parents, your youth leaders, and your relatives to protect yourself. Keeping your virginity until you marry is worth working for. It is a gift for your spouse and for your own happiness. Remember, however, not to try to do this in your own strength. Make Christ, and those He has given to you, your protection, wisdom, and strength. Then you will find happiness.

Unfortunately, some who read these pages have already "blown" it. Your hearts are already hurting and you wish you could restore your sexual purity. You may even have been drawn so far into the pit that you are disgusted with yourself. Yet, you find yourself powerless to break the habits that lie to you and cast you

141

down. You are under a power you can't resist. Perhaps you even wonder if there is any hope for you.

Yes, there is hope for you! You are not beyond the power of God's love and redemption in Jesus Christ. He is your hope. His power is much greater than the power you cannot resist. In your weakness His strength can be made perfect, but first you must face your weakness.

When, like an alcoholic who admits that he cannot resist booze, you confess that you are powerless to resist the lies that lead to sex, the outworking of Christ's power begins in you. Only be sure that Christ is living in you, and you are living in Christ. You can't resist the liar by trying to follow rules in your own strength. Your weakness must lead you to Christ, and Him alone. It is Christ who is stronger than satan, not you or me. So be sure that Christ lives in you.

The blood of Christ and the name of Jesus have authority over all in Heaven and earth. The spirits of darkness must obey His name. They cannot stop the cleansing power of His blood as it washes away all the filthiness of your sin and sets you free from the law of sin and death. Yes! The blood of Jesus breaks the curse of God on sin and removes any legal authority satan has gained through your sins to come in and torment you (Gal. 3:13). It seals all the windows through which the evil one would gain entrance to your soul.

Therefore, be assured that Jesus' arm is not too short to save you. His work is a complete work, restoring to you the purity and holiness you once possessed. With His sacrifice He has made you a pure bride, pouring out His life and blood for you.

If you have prayed to receive Christ, you belong to Him. He is your Husband. He accepts responsibility for you. Therefore, it is your obligation to do things that are pleasing to Him.

You cannot please Him in your own strength. Only as you admit your weakness and rely on His strength will you accomplish this task. Even your greatest weaknesses He can use for His glory. No failure is beyond His redemption. Take your weaknesses to Christ. He'll transform them—and you as well.

God will work through those who are in authority over you. Rebellion against your parents and other adults in your life is probably at the root of your sexual immorality. By removing yourself from their protection and refusing to be submissive to them, you opened yourself to deception and allowed yourself to be destroyed. Fix this problem. Apologize to your parents, your teachers, and any others God brings to mind, and change your direction. Expect to hear from God through them.

Test *everything* that doesn't come to you from your parents through two or three witnesses so that you will not be deceived again. Study God's Word and stay in fellowship with other believers who are studying the Bible and praying together. Discover how they can strengthen and support you, while you strengthen and support them. Plan to live as Christ's disciple for the rest of your life and make sure you can make future changes (of location, schools, employment, etc.) without breaking your discipleship under Christ within the fellowship of other believers.

Be particularly careful to avoid one-on-one dating with its built-in traps. Go in groups of three or four or more. Spend time helping people and letting them know that *they* are valuable. Don't just seek "romance."

If you have right relationships with many people your age, God can use them later for any purpose He wants, including marriage. Remember, however, that your weakness toward sex will probably make you untrustworthy for dating one-on-one for the rest of your life. Therefore, plan to protect yourself by seeking the company of other people, whether you are a girl or boy.

This may sound like bad news, but it is not. It is good news! Get used to giving up things to please your Savior. He will use it for your blessing.

Things to Think About

1. Do you believe that God is able to save and protect those who trust Him?

35

Eyes and Ears

This concluding chapter gives you a bit of a peak into the future. It's extra, but it is still based on God's design of men and women. Difficulties may arise even in good marriages that have avoided sexual immorality. If you are an older teen or a young married person, this information could help you in the future.

Keep these teachings in mind, put the Word of God in your heart, and seek to serve the Lord Jesus Christ. If you understand the Designer's goals in making men and women, you can avoid or solve many other problems. So let's review the overall design of men and women, and God's plan for their lives together, and look at an example of how girls and boys think and talk differently from each other—especially in the way they listen to words.

God's design of men as shields makes them think, see, and talk *externally*. In a similar manner, God's design of women as breasts causes them to think, see, and talk *internally*. What do we mean by this?

Because shields are designed and used to protect from external risks and threats—those that come from outside the home, city, etc.—men depend primarily upon sight to hunt, fight, and scout the enemy. Men also rely upon logic as they explain what they see, reason to solve problems, and plan their next steps. Thus, they are more likely to think and talk about *things* and *situations*. Men seldom worry about relationships because their thoughts are more consumed with fixing things than with relating to people.

Breasts have a completely different design from shields. Since their purpose is to nurture and strengthen relationships, women are the critical, internal ties that hold together their homes. As a woman relates to each individual member (husband-wife and mother-child), the family functions as a whole. Therefore, a woman looks beyond surface things and experiences to the deeper issues of health, attitudes, and relationships. What a woman *hears* is more significant than what she sees. She thinks and talks in terms of *people* and *relationships*. Thus, she tries to fix things using her perceptions of thoughts and meanings.

The whole design of men and women reveals this contrast between the internal and the external. Men find stimulation and fulfillment through their eyes; women relate and find fulfillment through their *ears*. Men are sexually stimulated *externally*; women are sexually stimulated *internally*. Men are turned on sexually by what they see; women are turned on sexually by what they *hear*. Men are fulfilled when they see results; women are satisfied when they *hear* words of thanks. A good paycheck does just fine to affirm a man; women depend upon praise for affirmation (Prov. 31:10-31). Men are deceived through their eyes; women are deceived through their *ears*. Women are most *heavily influenced by what they think a man's character is*, while men place more emphasis on external beauty. (This may be why God made women to be more beautiful than men and He said that "the woman is the glory of man" [1 Cor. 11:7b]. This may also be why God has instructed men to minister to their wives through the "washing of water with the word" [Eph. 5:26], and not the other way around.)

These fundamental differences are consistent. They extend throughout the design, thought, and behavior of men and women.

Although the differences may appear to be slight during the pre-teen and teen years, as men and women marry and assume their roles in the home and the world, the differences become more pronounced. These common characteristics of men and women have a direct effect on the way they talk to and hear each other—or rather, how they *talk at and don't hear* each other.

When a man talks to his wife, she does not listen primarily to the logic and facts that explain his point of view. She gets little information from logic and facts. No, she is listening to the meaning behind his words—the tone of his voice, the attitudes and state of his mind, the impact on relationships, the assigning and fulfilling of responsibilities. Her response to his words will, thus, be to see how she can solve the problems in those areas. With her thoughts thus focused, she may barely listen to her husband's logic or facts.

On the other hand, a woman who explains her feelings to her husband without supporting them with facts and reasonings frustrates him. He can't understand her or relate to her on those terms. He wants to know the specific things that made her feel that way, but sometimes she cannot tell him that. Oh, she may know what triggered her thoughts and feelings, but she cannot be certain whether that is the whole problem. Nor does she really care if it is or isn't.

Quite often, men and women will not remember a conversation the same way. This is particularly true in the midst of conflict, because conflict further complicates communication! For example, when a man says to his wife, "Why did you do this?" she may not respond by telling him the facts and logic that caused her to do what she did. This is especially true if she detects criticism in his question. Although the husband may not be criticizing but rather asking out of genuine interest, the wife may become defensive and respond from an emotional base instead of a logical base. She may have made her original decision the same way he would

147

have, but if she detects criticism, or conflict is openly present, she is not likely to explain it that way.

In this case, the woman often becomes more interested in "fixing the problem with her husband" than in dealing with the original issue. Therefore, her reaction may be one of several: She may propose something different. She may promise further action. She may apologize for her past decision. In any case, she will go straight to the root of the problem from her perspective and probably will not respond to the matter from her husband's standpoint. Although her husband may often be really interested in understanding what her *reasoning* was at the time of her action, she will fail to explain *why* she did a particular thing. *In other words, the woman will respond to the perceived distress in her husband's voice, not to his literal words.*

Is it surprising, then, that marital conflict is so prevalent? Most questions can be interpreted at least two ways. Voice tone communicates more than words. The more frustrated and insistent a man becomes to get a woman to answer logically (as he sees it), the more concerned she will become to solve the relationship problem. In the end, neither one hears the other.

This is only a tiny example typical of much communication between husbands and wives. You undoubtedly have heard similar conversations between your parents. This pattern has created a tendency among women to think men are "less sensitive" than women because men don't see, think, or talk about things as "deeply" as women. It would be unwise, though, to make a value judgment of "good" or "bad" on this. Women and men simply think, talk, and observe differently.

Although men do look at things more externally than women, this doesn't mean that their beliefs and convictions are superficial. In fact, their thoughts and opinions focus outward more than inward because God gave them the "outside" job and created them to excel in it. It may be just as frustrating for a man to see that his wife can't understand from his viewpoint, as it is for a woman to see that her husband is incapable of appreciating hers. Neither one is necessarily insensitive to the other. They just look at things from different perspectives.

Men and women are different because God created them that way. Indeed, this is a positive gift because they are each suited to different roles within the family, and one can see things the other can't.

We are all incomplete. Both the husband and the wife are God's gift to complete the other. The woman who thinks her husband is insensitive because he doesn't seem to understand her inner needs could easily think quite differently when the alarm goes off and a burglar enters the house in the middle of the night. The fact that she feels secure under his protection is the main thing that enables her to be a happy woman, not how great or inadequate he may be in grasping her inmost thoughts. The same is true of the man who is well nurtured by his wife.

The Word of God and many other books contain other valuable information about the dissimilarities between men and women and the benefits marriage partners can attain from those differences. It is not necessary that teens understand all this stuff now. What is necessary is that the teen commit himself (or herself) to the Lord's plan so that marriage will be rich and fulfilling. Then the Lord will work these things out between you and the partner He has for you, as you both submit to Him. Because God's love is in your love for your marriage partner, and He has the knowledge and power to change both of you so that you can meet each other's needs, you can confidently face the future. Yes, you will need to change, but God is in the changing business!

Girls, prepare yourselves now for your wedding day, when your girlhood dreams will be fulfilled. As you come together with your bridegroom for the first time, his words will be true! Make yourself ready in purity. *Protect your ears.* Your knight is coming! Stay under protection until the dragon in slain and the castle is scaled.

149

Guys, protect yourselves by seeing girls that are under a man's protection. Also make a covenant to *protect your eyes* (Job 31:1). If you discover in your heart that you love your girl and she is worth any price, you will not be disappointed. After you have worked for her, protected her, and waited for her, you will "see [the results] and be satisfied" (Is. 53:11) when you come together on your wedding night—and for the rest of your life.

God has spoken. He who has spoken is faithful to fulfill all He has promised. Young men and young women, *you will be satisfied.*

Epilogue: Summary

God has provided for our completion in Jesus Christ, who is God's only solution for sin. He alone can bring us into God's presence and restore our relationship as God's sons and daughters. He is the only means by which we can know total wholeness and fulfillment. The many important features God has built into boys and girls are part of His plan to help them enjoy fulfilled lives that portray the gospel of Jesus Christ. His provisions for sex and reproduction are chief among these.

Those who misuse God's provision suffer loss and destruction. The pain of their impurity follows them throughout life unless they find restoration through Jesus Christ. The ruination of people and marriages caused by sexual sin includes the following penalties:

- Sexual immorality leads to increased insecurity in a girl and the mounting of strongholds that war against men. No level of economic wealth or expression of love from her husband will ever satisfy the appetite of the immoral woman for more security and love.

- Sexual immorality destroys the ability of a girl to be soul-bonded to a man. Therefore, she will be unable to find

151

fulfillment in her marriage. Instead, she will live only for herself and her children.

- Sexual immorality brings the spirit of harlotry into a girl, whereby she uses sex as a means of getting what she needs. Sex, thus, becomes a means of winning or of controlling men in a useless attempt to gain increased security in her relationships.

- Sexual immorality destroys wisdom and reduces a boy's capacity to defend and protect girls. Such boys will later prove to be insufficient in protecting and providing for their families.

- Sexual immorality causes boys to have more and more of an appetite for sex, which can never be satisfied. In time this appetite will lead him to sexual perversions and abominations. No level of nurture or expression of love by his wife will ever satisfy him.

- Sexual immorality causes a boy to try to buy sex by extending favors, buying presents, or in some other manner showing that he loves his girl or his wife. Sex later becomes a trade rather than a freewill offering of love to his marriage partner.

- Sexual immorality prevents a boy from bonding to a girl he really loves because it enables him to avoid paying a soul-price for her. Abstaining from sex and being kept under the strong authority of someone stronger who is protecting the girl is the best way to guarantee that a boy will bond to a girl before marriage.

Our society has led many young people to believe that sex before marriage does them no harm. In truth, pre-marital sex has led to much destruction that the secular world does not understand. Today many boys never marry. Girls wonder why. The sad truth is that sex is so readily available that there is no need for men to pay the high price a successful marriage requires. Such boys are unable to handle the responsibility of marriage. Even if they do marry, divorce or years of marital strife often follow. The man cannot find contentment with his wife, neither can he deal wisely with the strongholds that separate him from her. Meanwhile, his wife often experiences the same dilemma. There is no bonding to force a search for wisdom. There is no bonding to withstand the temptations and trials.

We live in a spirit world in which the forces of satan have been allowed to retain considerable power until the time when Christ banishes the forces of wickedness forever. For those who are not called by Christ, there is no hope. For those who know Him, He provides the greatest protection available to this generation of sons and daughters. Our youth can avoid the pitfalls of sexual sin. Jesus Christ has power over all sin. His gift of salvation reaches to the ends of the earth.

May God's grace through Jesus Christ our Savior and Lord be in abundance to all who read these pages. Amen.

Books by Karl Duff

- *Restoration of Marriage*: An unusually deep and scripturally thorough study of gender characteristics, gender "strongholds," and the increasing difficulties and warfare these produce in marriage. Includes a section of testimonies on the functions of men to protect wives and daughters, father-daughter relationships, restoring marriages, and God's providing the promised Bridegroom.

- *Restoration of Men (God's Rescue of Women and Children)*: God provides healing, restoration, and protective accountability for men who find themselves ineffectual as husbands and fathers.

- *Lord and Scoutmaster*: The author relates humorous as well as educational true life adventures he had as a Scout and then as a Scoutmaster.

- *Leader's Guide for High Adventure*: This is a booklet of practical tips for leading Scouts or youth groups on extended backpacking or canoeing trips, based upon three decades of experience.

- *Still the Master of the Sea*: With signs and wonders God intervened in a modern hydrofoil warship program and changed a prideful naval officer. A remarkable testimony of miracles.

- *Dating, Intimacy & the Teenage Years*: God's design of male-female relationships is an important part of His plan for our lives. Youth must obey God's plan to find happiness and fulfillment. Includes discussion questions.

To order additional books, contact the author at:

Karl Duff
6112 Wynn Jones Road East
Port Orchard, WA 98366
206.871.1265

Place this order form in an envelope along with your check or money order.

Quantity	Description	Unit Price	Total Price
	Restoration of Marriage	$13.95	
	Restoration of Men	$ 9.95	
	Lord and Scoutmaster	$ 8.95	
	Leaders' Guide for High Adventure	$ 3.00	
	Still the Master of the Sea	$10.95	
	Dating, Intimacy & the Teenage Years	$11.99	

Ship. (quant.)	1-2	3-5	6-9	10-14	15-19	20-25
Ship. Cost	$2.50	4.00	6.50	10.50	13.25	16.00

Subtotal

Less Discount

Plus Shipping

TOTAL DUE

Name: _____

Address: _____

City/State/Zip: _____   Phone # _____

Signature: _____   Date: _____

20% Discount for 5 or more copies

Books to help you grow strong in Jesus

━━━ **LADY IN WAITING**

by Debby Jones and Jackie Kendall.

This is not just another book for single women! The authors, both well-known conference speakers, present an in-depth study on the biblical Ruth that reveals the characteristics every woman of God should develop. Learn how you can become a lady of faith,
purity, contentment, patience—and much more—as you pursue a personal and intimate
relationship with your Lord Jesus!

ISBN 1-56043-848-7

Devotional Journal and Study Guide

ISBN 1-56043-298-5

━━━ **FROM THE FATHER'S HEART**

by Charles Slagle.

This is a beautiful look at the true heart of your heavenly Father. Through these sensitive
selections that include short love notes, letters, and prophetic words from God to His children, you will develop the kind of closeness and intimacy with the loving Father that you
have always longed for. From words of encouragement and inspiration to words of gentle
correction, each letter addresses times that we all experience. For those who diligently
seek God, you will recognize Him in these pages.

ISBN 0-914903-82-9

━━━ **AN INVITATION TO FRIENDSHIP**: From the Father's Heart, Volume 2

by Charles Slagle.

Our God is a Father whose heart longs for His children to sit and talk with Him in fellowship and oneness. This second volume of intimate letters from the Father to you, His
child, reveals His passion, dreams, and love for you. As you read them, you will find yourself drawn ever closer within the circle of His embrace. The touch of His presence will
change your life forever!

ISBN 0-7684-2013-X

━━━ **DON'T DIE IN THE WINTER...**

by Dr. Millicent Thompson.

Why do we go through hard times? Why must we suffer pain? In *Don't Die in the Winter...* Dr. Thompson, a pastor, teacher, and conference speaker, explains the spiritual sea-
sons and cycles that people experience. A spiritual winter is simply a season that tests our
growth. We need to endure our winters, for in the plan of God, spring always follows
winter!

ISBN 1-56043-558-5

━━━ **UNDERSTANDING THE DREAMS YOU DREAM**

by Ira Milligan.

Have you ever had a dream in which you think God was speaking to you? Here is a practical guide, from the Christian perspective, for understanding the symbolic language of
dreams. Deliberately written without technical jargon, this book can be easily understood
and used by everyone. Includes a complete dictionary of symbols.

ISBN 1-56043-284-5

Available at your local Christian bookstore.

**For more information and sample chapters,
visit www.reapernet.com**

Titles that will challenge & encourage you!

━ SECRET SOURCES OF POWER
by T.F. Tenney with Tommy Tenney.

Everyone is searching for power. People are longing for some external force to empower their lives and transform their circumstances. *Secret Sources of Power* furnishes some of the keys that will unlock the door to Divine power. You might be surprised at what is on the other side of that door. It will be the opposite of the world's concepts of power and how to obtain it. You will discover that before you lay hold of God's power you must let go of your own resources. You will be challenged to go down before you can be lifted up. Death always comes before resurrection. If you are dissatisfied with your life and long for the power of God to be manifested in you then now is the time. Take the keys and open the door to *Secret Sources of Power*!
ISBN 0-7684-5000-4

━ THE GOD CHASERS (National Best-Seller)
by Tommy Tenney.

There are those so hungry, so desperate for His presence, that they become consumed with finding Him. Their longing for Him moves them to do what they would otherwise never do: Chase God. But what does it really mean to chase God? Can He be "caught"? Is there an end to the thirsting of man's soul for Him? Meet Tommy Tenney—God chaser. Join him in his search for God. Follow him as he ignores the maze of religious tradition and finds himself, not chasing God, but to his utter amazement, caught by the One he had chased.
ISBN 0-7684-2016-4
Also available in Spanish
ISBN 0-7899-0642-2

━ GOD CHASERS DAILY MEDITATION & PERSONAL JOURNAL
by Tommy Tenney.
ISBN 0-7684-2040-7

━ THE POWER OF BROKENNESS
by Don Nori.

Accepting Brokenness is a must for becoming a true vessel of the Lord, and is a stepping-stone to revival in our hearts, our homes, and our churches. Brokenness alone brings us to the wonderful revelation of how deep and great our Lord's mercy really is. Join this companion who leads us through the darkest of nights. Discover the *Power of Brokenness*.
ISBN 1-56043-178-4

━ SECRETS OF THE MOST HOLY PLACE
by Don Nori.

Here is a prophetic parable you will read again and again. The winds of God are blowing, drawing you to His Life within the Veil of the Most Holy Place. There you begin to see as you experience a depth of relationship your heart has yearned for. This book is a living, dynamic experience with God!
ISBN 1-56043-076-1

Available at your local Christian bookstore.

For more information and sample chapters, visit www.reapernet.com

Foundationally Spirit-filled. Biblically Sound. Spiritually Inspirational.

━━ THE LOST PASSIONS OF JESUS

by Donald L. Milam, Jr.

What motivated Jesus to pursue the cross? What inner strength kept His feet on the path laid before Him? Time and tradition have muted the Church's knowledge of the passions that burned in Jesus' heart, but if we want to—if we dare to—we can still seek those same passions. Learn from a close look at Jesus' own life and words and from the writings of other dedicated followers the passions that enflamed the Son of God and changed the world forever!

ISBN 0-9677402-0-7

━━ THE ASCENDED LIFE

by Bernita J. Conway.

A believer does not need to wait until Heaven to experience an intimate relationship with the Lord. When you are born again, your life becomes His, and He pours His life into yours. Here Bernita Conway explains from personal study and experience the truth of "abiding in the Vine," the Lord Jesus Christ. When you grasp this understanding and begin to walk in it, it will change your whole life and relationship with your heavenly Father!

ISBN 1-56043-337-X

━━ THE MARTYRS' TORCH

by Bruce Porter.

In every age of history, darkness has threatened to extinguish the light. But also in every age of history, heroes and heroines of the faith rose up to hold high the torch of their testimony—witnesses to the truth of the gospel of Jesus Christ. On a fateful spring day at Columbine High, others lifted up their torches and joined the crimson path of the martyrs' way. We cannot forget their sacrifice. A call is sounding forth from Heaven: "Who will take up the martyrs' torch which fell from these faithful hands?" Will you?

ISBN 0-7684-2046-6

Available at your local Christian bookstore.

For more information and sample chapters, visit www.reapernet.com